Favourite
Cupcakes
and Cheesecakes

Published by:
R&R Publications Marketing Pty. Ltd
ABN 78 348 105 138
PO Box 254, Carlton North, Victoria 3054 Australia
Phone (61 3) 9381 2199 Fax (61 3) 9381 2689
E-mail: info@randrpublications.com.au
Website: www.randrpublications.com.au
Australia wide toll free: 1800 063 296

©Anthony Carroll

Favourite Cupcakes and Cheesecakes

Publisher: Anthony Carroll
Production Manager: Neil Hargreaves
Designer: Aisling Gallagher, Elain Wei Voon Loh
Food Editor: Neil Hargreaves
Food Stylist: Lee Blaylock, Sebastian Sedlak, Neil Hargreaves
Food Photography: Brent Parker Jones, R&R Photstudio
Recipe Development: James Freer, John Quai Hoi, R&R Test Kitchen, Sebastian Sedlak,
Neil Hargreaves
Proofreader: Stephen Jones, Vanessa Battersby

Disclaimer: The nutritional information listed with each recipe is calculated on a per serve basis and
does not include the nutrient content of garnishes or any accompaniments not listed in specific
quantities in the ingredient list. The nutritional information for each recipe is an estimate only, and
may vary depending on the brand of ingredients used, and due to natural biological variations in
the composition of natural foods such as meat, fish, fruit and vegetables. The nutritional information
was calculated by using the computer program Foodworks dietary analysis software (version 3.01,
Xyris Software Pty. Ltd. Queensland Australia), and is based on the Australian food composition
tables and food manufacturers' data. Where not specified, ingredients are always analysed as
average or medium, not small or large.

ISBN 978-1-74022-676-9

First Edition Printed June 2008
Second Edition Printed May 2009
This Edition Printed August 2009
Computer Typeset in Futura

Printed in Singapore

Contents

Introduction

Welcome back

These traditional little snacks of celebration have recently crept back into our list of daily favourites; the sweet breakfast muffin has to move over to leave some room for its forebear, the cupcake!

There was a time when the cheery little fellow called the cupcake was out of favour: a bit nanna, a bit tizzy tea-time, a bit doily and old lace, sweet and indulgent in all the old-fashioned ways. Those days are over as we go back and appreciate what is good about traditional fare.

In this book we will guide you through some basic and some more exotic cupcake bases and offer some simple and some more complicated topping suggestions. Remember that you can mix and match: combine a cupcake base that takes your fancy with a different topping, and then decorate in yet another way! All of the techniques given are have been created so that they are achievable by the novice, and offer a range of ideas and flavour combinations to broaden the scope of a more experienced baker. Surprise those around you with sweet treats in the lunch box or playful snacks for after school, or even cluster cupcakes on a tiered stand for a fashionable centrepiece to a wedding breakfast.

In today's market there are many specialty products available for the baker. Cake decorations and sugar art pieces are a great example: pre-made pieces can be a useful short cuts that can crown a homemade baking achievement for a minimal amount of effort with maximum effect.

Most specialty stores for cake decorating usually also stock sugar art decorations in a wide range of themes. These can be found in most cities or online, and also generally transport easily as they need no refrigeration.

Experiment for yourself, but remember to be conservative with your cake adjustments if experimenting and write down your ingredients and quantity changes as you go. Be a little freer when adjusting and experimenting with icings and butter cream topping, and be as loose and abstract as you can feel like when it comes to topping your creations. Crumble or chop up chocolate bars and sweet treats: don't just use your supermarket for inspiration here, remember the desserts of all nations that you find at the delicatessens and food markets in your local area. All of these things are fair game in the world of decorating your individual treasures. Honeycomb, fairy floss, Turkish Delight, nougats: the list is endless. All of these can be cut, crumbled or piled high on top of your sweet creations. Be guided by your imagination and sense of adventure. You will soon have entirely individual cup cakes that you alone have created.

Good Luck and Get Baking!

Making a paper piping bag

1 Cut a 25 cm square of greaseproof paper. Cut the square in half diagonally to form two triangles.

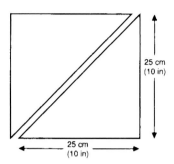

2 To make the piping bag, place the paper triangles on top of each other and mark the three corners A, B and C.

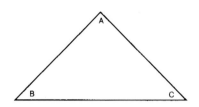

3 Fold corner B around and inside corner A.

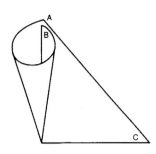

4 Bring corner C around the outside of the bag until it fits exactly behind corner A. At this stage all three corners should be together and the point closed.

 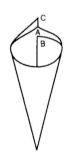

5 Fold corner A over two or three times to hold the bag together. Snip the point off the bag and drop into an icing nozzle. The piping bag can also be used without a nozzle for writing and outlines, in which case only the very tip of the point should be snipped off.

We have included the basic explanation for how to prepare a piping bag. It is a handy skill if you have a piece of baking paper around, but if you find it a bit fiddly or if you don't have any paper on hand, the back-up trick is to fill the corner of a small plastic bag, simply roll it up and snip off the point. As long as the bag is sturdy enough and the person controlling the piping is gentle enough, the humble plastic bag can work wonderfully for applying line decorations or writing messages on individual cakes.

Preparing a plastic bag for piping

1

2

3

Icing

Icing

Icing

Vanilla
Cupcakes

There is something quaint and reassuring about the use of vanilla in a recipe, it is the great pacifier of all flavouring and marries well with white chocolate, creating dainty cupcake treats.

Persian Vanilla Cupcakes

Preparation 12 mins **Cooking** 20 mins **Calories** 500 **Fat** 35g **Carbohydrate** 44g

3 eggs
½ cup butter, softened
1 cup caster sugar
½ cup milk
1½ cups self-raising flour, sifted
1 teaspoon vanilla extract

Topping
1½ cups icing sugar
1 teaspoon lemon essence
1 teaspoon vanilla extract
½ cup butter, room temperature
Persian fairy floss

1   Preheat the oven to 160°C. Line a 12-cupcake pan with cupcake papers. In a medium-sized bowl, lightly beat the eggs, add butter and sugar, then mix until light and fluffy.

2   Add milk, flour and vanilla, and stir to combine. Beat with an electric mixer for 2 minutes, until light and creamy.

3   Divide the mixture evenly between the cake papers. Bake for 18–20 minutes until risen and firm to touch. Allow to cool for a few minutes and then transfer to a wire rack. Allow to cool fully before icing.

Topping

1   Meanwhile, combine all topping ingredients except fairy floss, mix with a wooden spoon until well combined, and beat with the spoon until light and fluffy.

2   Place mixture into a piping bag with a star-shaped nozzle and pipe onto all cupcakes. Top with fairy floss.

Makes 12

Vanilla Rose Cupcakes

Preparation 12 mins **Cooking** 20 mins **Calories** 483 **Fat** 35g **Carbohydrate** 42g

3 eggs
½ cup butter, softened
1 cup caster sugar
½ cup milk
1½ cups self-raising flour, sifted
1 teaspoon vanilla extract

Topping
1½ cups icing sugar
1 teaspoon rose water
½ cup butter, room temperature
6 drops vanilla extract
miniature dried roses,
approximately 8 per cupcake
(available from specialty cake
decoration stores)

1 Preheat the oven to 160°C. Line a 12-cupcake pan with cupcake papers. In a medium-sized bowl, lightly beat the eggs, add butter and sugar, then mix until light and fluffy.

2 Add milk, flour and vanilla, and stir to combine. Beat with an electric mixer for 2 minutes, until light and creamy.

3 Divide the mixture evenly between the cake papers. Bake for 18–20 minutes until risen and firm to touch. Allow to cool for a few minutes and then transfer to a wire rack. Allow to cool fully before icing.

Topping

1 Meanwhile, combine half of all the topping ingredients except roses, mix with a wooden spoon, add remaining ingredients and beat with the spoon until light and fluffy. Place mixture into a piping bag with a plain nozzle and pipe onto cupcakes. Decorate with roses.

Makes 12

Baby Violet Cupcakes

Preparation 12 mins **Cooking** 20 mins **Calories** 329 **Fat** 18g **Carbohydrate** 39g

3 eggs
½ cup butter, softened
1 cup caster sugar
½ cup milk
1½ cups self-raising flour, sifted
1 teaspoon vanilla extract

Topping
1½ cups icing sugar
½ cup butter, room temperature
1 tablespoon water
6 drops purple food colouring
3 teaspoon coloured sugar sprinkles
12 miniature baby rattle toys

1 Preheat the oven to 160°C. Line a 12-cup cake pan, with cup cake papers. In a medium-sized bowl lightly beat the eggs, add butter and sugar, then mix until light and fluffy.

2 Add milk, flour and vanilla, and stir to combine. Beat with an electric mixer for 2 minutes, until light and creamy.

3 Divide the mixture evenly between the cake papers. Bake for 18–20 minutes until risen and firm to touch. Allow to cool for a few minutes and then transfer to a wire rack. Allow to cool fully before icing.

Topping

1 Meanwhile, combine the topping ingredients, and mix with a wooden spoon. Using the back of a teaspoon, apply the topping to cupcakes. Top each cupcake with purple sugar sprinkles and top with novelty toy.

Makes 12

Vanilla Butter Cupcakes

Preparation 12 mins **Cooking** 20 mins **Calories** 487 **Fat** 35g **Carbohydrate** 42g

3 eggs
½ cup butter, softened
1 cup caster sugar
½ cup buttermilk
1½ cups self-raising flour, sifted
1 teaspoon vanilla extract

Topping
1½ cups icing sugar
½ cup butter, room temperature
6 drops vanilla extract
coloured confectionary sprinkles
(available from cake
decoration stores)

1 Preheat the oven to 160°C. Line a 12-cupcake pan with cupcake papers. In a medium-sized bowl, lightly beat the eggs, add butter and sugar, then mix until light and fluffy.
2 Add buttermilk, flour and vanilla, and stir to combine. Beat with an electric mixer for 2 minutes, until light and creamy.
3 Divide the mixture evenly between the cake papers. Bake for 18–20 minutes until risen and firm to touch. Allow to cool for a few minutes and then transfer to a wire rack. Allow to cool fully before icing.

Topping
1 Meanwhile, combine half the topping ingredients except sprinkles, and mix with a wooden spoon until mixed together, add remaining ingredients and beat with the spoon until light and fluffy.
2 Spoon topping onto cakes using the back of a spoon. Decorate with coloured sprinkles.

Makes 12

Lavender Buttercream Cupcakes

Preparation 12 mins **Cooking** 20 mins **Calories** 487 **Fat** 35g **Carbohydrate** 42g

3 eggs
½ cup butter, softened
1 cup caster sugar
½ cup milk
1½ cups self-raising flour, sifted
1 teaspoon vanilla extract

Topping
1½ cups icing sugar
1 teaspoon lavender essence
½ cup butter, room temperature
2 drops purple food colouring
candied lavender (available from cake decoration stores)

1 Preheat the oven to 160°C. Line a 12-cupcake pan with cupcake papers. In a medium-sized bowl, lightly beat the eggs, add butter and sugar, then mix until light and fluffy.

2 Add milk, flour and vanilla, and stir to combine. Beat with an electric mixer for 2 minutes, until light and creamy.

3 Divide the mixture evenly between the cake papers. Bake for 18–20 minutes until risen and firm to touch. Allow to cool for a few minutes and then transfer to a wire rack. Allow to cool fully before icing.

Topping

1 Meanwhile, combine half the topping ingredients except candied lavender, mix with a wooden spoon, add remaining ingredients and beat with a whisk until light and fluffy.

2 Apply the topping with the back of a teaspoon or a small spatula. Place the candied lavender on top.

Makes 12

White Chocolate and Buttermilk Cupcakes

Preparation 12 mins **Cooking** 20 mins **Calories** 489 **Fat** 33g **Carbohydrate** 45g

3 eggs
½ cup butter, softened
1 cup caster sugar
½ cup buttermilk
1½ cups self-raising flour, sifted
1 teaspoon vanilla extract

Topping
100g white chocolate,
coarsely grated
1 tablespoon butter
⅓ cup cream, thickened
candied frangipanis (available from
cake decoration stores)

1 Preheat the oven to 160°C. Line a 12-cupcake pan with cupcake papers. In a medium-sized bowl, lightly beat the eggs, add butter and sugar, then mix until light and fluffy.

2 Add buttermilk, flour and vanilla, and stir to combine. Beat with an electric mixer for 2 minutes, until light and creamy.

3 Divide the mixture evenly between the cake papers. Bake for 18–20 minutes until risen and firm to touch. Allow to cool for a few minutes and then transfer to a wire rack. Allow to cool fully before icing.

Topping

1 Meanwhile, combine the chocolate and butter in a medium-sized saucepan over a medium heat. As the mixture begins to melt, add the cream slowly, then reduce heat to low, stirring constantly, until mixture thickens.

2 Remove from heat and cool. Spread evenly onto cupcakes with a teaspoon and then top with frangipani decorations.

Makes 12

Marshmallow Vanilla Buttercups

Preparation 12 mins **Cooking** 20 mins **Calories** 412 **Fat** 25g **Carbohydrate** 45g

3 eggs
½ cup butter, softened
1 cup caster sugar
½ cup buttermilk
1 ½ cups self-raising flour, sifted
2 teaspoons vanilla extract

Topping
100g icing sugar
½ cup butter, room temperature
1 teaspoon vanilla extract
marshmallow dots (100g minimum)

1 Preheat the oven to 160°C. Line a 12-cupcake pan with cupcake papers. In a medium-sized bowl, lightly beat the eggs, add butter and sugar, then mix until light and fluffy.

2 Add buttermilk, flour and vanilla, and stir to combine. Beat with an electric mixer for 2 minutes, until light and creamy.

3 Divide the mixture evenly between the cake papers. Bake for 18–20 minutes until risen and firm to touch. Allow to cool for a few minutes and then transfer to a wire rack. Allow to cool fully before icing.

Topping

1 Meanwhile, combine half the icing sugar and butter, mix with a wooden spoon, add remaining icing sugar, butter and vanilla extract and beat with the spoon until light and fluffy.

2 Add dollop (tablespoon-size) of topping to the centre of each cake. Make a flower design with the small marshmallows in the centre of each cupcake.

Makes 12

Double White Cupcakes

Preparation 12 mins **Cooking** 20 mins **Calories** 568 **Fat** 37g **Carbohydrate** 56g

3 eggs
½ cup butter, softened
1 cup caster sugar
½ cup milk
1½ cups self-raising flour, sifted
100g white chocolate, grated
1 teaspoon vanilla extract

Topping
1½ cups icing sugar
½ cup butter, room temperature
72 silver balls
72 pre-made meringue decorations

1 Preheat the oven to 160°C. Line a 12-cupcake pan with cupcake papers. In a medium-sized bowl, lightly beat the eggs, add butter and sugar, then mix until light and fluffy.

2 Add the milk, flour, chocolate and vanilla, and stir to combine. Beat with an electric mixer for 2 minutes, until light and creamy.

3 Divide the mixture evenly between the cake papers. Bake for 18–20 minutes until risen and firm to touch. Allow to cool for a few minutes and then transfer to a wire rack. Allow to cool fully before icing.

Topping

1 Meanwhile, combine half the icing sugar and butter, mix with a wooden spoon, add the remaining icing sugar and butter and beat with the spoon until light and fluffy. Spoon onto cupcakes, leaving a little aside.

2 Using a dab of butter cream, place a silver ball at the centre of each meringue, and then place them around each cupcake.

Makes 12

Buttermilk Booty Cupcakes

Preparation 12 mins **Cooking** 20 mins **Calories** 488 **Fat** 33.5g **Carbohydrate** 42g

3 eggs
½ cup butter, softened
1 cup caster sugar
½ cup milk
1½ cups self-raising flour, sifted
1 teaspoon vanilla extract

Topping
1½ cups icing sugar
½ cup butter, room temperature
blue and pink food colouring
baby booties (available from specialty cake decoration stores)

1 Preheat the oven to 160°C. Line a 12-cupcake pan with cupcake papers. In a medium-sized bowl, lightly beat the eggs, add butter and sugar, then mix until light and fluffy.

2 Add milk, flour and vanilla, and stir to combine. Beat with an electric mixer for 2 minutes, until light and creamy.

3 Divide the mixture evenly between the cake papers. Bake for 18–20 minutes until risen and firm to touch. Allow to cool for a few minutes and then transfer to a wire rack. Allow to cool fully before icing.

Topping

1 Meanwhile, combine half the icing sugar and butter, mix with a wooden spoon, add the remaining icing sugar and butter and beat with the spoon until light and fluffy.

2 Divide the topping into two bowls, and add blue food colouring and pink to the other. Spread the topping evenly onto cupcakes and then top with baby booties.

Makes 12

White Musk Cupcakes

Preparation 12 mins **Cooking** 20 mins **Calories** 492 **Fat** 40g **Carbohydrate** 43g

3 eggs
½ cup butter, softened
1 cup caster sugar
½ cup milk
1½ cups self-raising flour, sifted
1 teaspoon vanilla extract
6 drops rose water

Topping
1½ cups icing sugar
½ cup butter, room temperature
6 drops rose water
small quantity of musk sticks,
cut into slices

1. Preheat the oven to 160°C. Line a 12-cupcake pan with cupcake papers. In a medium-sized bowl, lightly beat the eggs, add butter and sugar, and mix until light and fluffy.
2. Add milk, flour, vanilla and rose water, and stir to combine. Beat with an electric mixer for 2 minutes, until light and creamy.
3. Divide the mixture evenly between the cake papers. Bake for 18–20 minutes until risen and firm to touch. Allow to cool for a few minutes and then transfer to a wire rack. Allow to cool fully before icing.

Topping

1. Meanwhile, combine all the topping ingredients except musk stick pieces in a small bowl, mix with a wooden spoon until well combined, then whisk until light and fluffy.
2. Place mixture into a piping bag with a star-shaped nozzle and pipe onto all cupcakes. Top with slices of musk sticks.

Makes 12

Triple White Cupcakes

Preparation 12 mins **Cooking** 20 mins **Calories** 679 **Fat** 50g **Carbohydrate** 56g

3 eggs
½ cup butter, softened
1 cup caster sugar
½ cup milk
1½ cups self-raising flour, sifted
1 teaspoon vanilla extract
100g white chocolate, chopped

Topping
200g white chocolate buttons
⅓ cup cream, thickened
½ cup butter, room temperature
1 cup icing sugar

1 Preheat the oven to 160°C. Line a 12-cupcake pan with cupcake papers. In a medium-sized bowl, lightly beat the eggs, add butter and sugar, then mix until light and fluffy.

2 Add milk, flour and vanilla, and stir to combine. Beat with an electric mixer for 2 minutes, until light and creamy. Add white chocolate and stir through the mixture.

3 Divide the mixture evenly between the cake papers. Bake for 18–20 minutes until risen and firm to touch. Allow to cool for a few minutes and then transfer to a wire rack. Allow to cool fully before icing.

Topping

1 Meanwhile, combine 160g of the white chocolate with cream in a medium-sized saucepan over a medium heat. As the mixture begins to melt, reduce heat to low, stirring constantly, until mixture thickens. Remove from heat and cool.

2 Combine butter and icing sugar, and mix with a wooden spoon. Beat with the spoon until light and fluffy. Add melted chocolate, combine, then spoon onto cupcakes. Top with remaining white chocolate buttons.

Makes 12

Vanilla Heart Cupcakes

Preparation 12 mins   **Cooking** 20 mins   **Calories** 314   **Fat** 18g   **Carbohydrate** 35g

3 eggs
½ cup butter, softened
1 cup caster sugar
½ cup milk
1½ cups self-raising flour, sifted
1 teaspoon vanilla extract
100g white chocolate, chopped

Topping
⅓ cup icing sugar
2 tablespoons water
⅓ cup seedless strawberry jam
heart-shaped candles

1 Preheat the oven to 160°C. Line a 12-cupcake pan with cupcake papers. In a medium-sized bowl, lightly beat the eggs, add butter and sugar, then mix until light and fluffy.

2 Add milk, flour and vanilla, and stir to combine. Beat with an electric mixer for 2 minutes, until light and creamy. Add white chocolate and stir through the mixture.

3 Divide the mixture evenly between the cake papers. Bake for 18–20 minutes until risen and firm to touch. Allow to cool for a few minutes and then transfer to a wire rack. Allow to cool fully before icing.

Topping
1 Meanwhile, combine icing sugar and water in a small bowl. Add strawberry jam to a piping bag using the smallest nozzle, and pipe over the cake. Repeat with white icing. Top with heart-shaped candle.

Makes 12

Vanilla Sprinkle Cupcakes

Preparation 12 mins **Cooking** 20 mins **Calories** 482 **Fat** 35g **Carbohydrate** 42g

3 eggs
½ cup butter, softened
1 cup caster sugar
½ cup milk
1½ cups self-raising flour, sifted
1 teaspoon vanilla extract
1 teaspoon cocoa powder

Topping
½ cup icing sugar
¾ tablespoon hot water
sprinkles (or 100s & 1000s)

1 Preheat the oven to 160°C. Line a 12-cupcake pan with cupcake papers. In a medium-sized bowl, lightly beat the eggs, add butter and sugar, then mix until light and fluffy.

2 Add milk, flour and vanilla, and stir to combine. Beat with an electric mixer for 2 minutes, until light and creamy.

3 Divide the mixture in half, and add the vanilla to one half and cocoa powder to the other, and divide evenly between the cake papers. Bake for 18–20 minutes until risen and firm to touch. Allow to cool for a few minutes and then transfer to a wire rack. Allow to cool fully before icing.

Topping

1 Meanwhile, combine icing sugar and water in a small bowl, and mix with a wooden spoon. Spoon onto cupcakes. Tip sprinkles onto a small plate and gently press each cupcake into the sprinkles.

Makes 12

Butterfly Cupcakes

Preparation 12 mins **Cooking** 20 mins **Calories** 487 **Fat** 35g **Carbohydrate** 42g

3 eggs
½ cup butter, softened
1 cup caster sugar
½ cup milk
1½ cups self-raising flour, sifted
1 teaspoon vanilla extract

Topping
1½ cups icing sugar
1 teaspoon vanilla extract
½ cup butter, room temperature

1 Preheat the oven to 160°C. Line a 12-cupcake pan with cup cake papers. In a medium-sized bowl, lightly beat the eggs, add butter and sugar, then mix until light and fluffy.

2 Add milk, flour and vanilla, and stir to combine. Beat with an electric mixer for 2 minutes, until light and creamy.

3 Divide the mixture evenly between the cake papers. Bake for 18–20 minutes until risen and firm to touch. Allow to cool for a few minutes and then transfer to a wire rack. Allow to cool fully before icing.

Topping

1 Meanwhile, combine all topping ingredients, mix with a wooden spoon until well combined, then beat with the spoon until light and fluffy.

2 Place mixture into a piping bag, and set aside. Using a sharp knife, cut a 10cm circle into the centre of each cupcake, slicing the top off. Cut these circles in half and set aside. Fill the centre of each cupcake with icing, and stand the two pieces of cake top upright, to form wings.

Makes 12

Chocolate Cupcakes

Chocolate is the perfect ingredient for desserts and cupcakes, and deserving of its own chapter. Watch your family gather around as you pipe on lashings of rich chocolate ganache, creating a treat that is hard to pass up.

Butter Choc Cupcakes

Preparation 12 mins   **Cooking** 20 mins   **Calories** 500   **Fat** 35g   **Carbohydrate** 44g

3 eggs
1 cup butter, softened
1 cup caster sugar
½ cup buttermilk
1½ cups self-raising flour, sifted
1 teaspoon cocoa powder
1 teaspoon vanilla extract
½ cup milk chocolate pieces, finely chopped
⅓ cup pure cream

Topping
1½ cups icing sugar
½ cup butter, room temperature
5 drops pink food colouring
sugar flowers (available from cake decoration shops)

1   Preheat the oven to 160°C. Line a 12-cupcake pan with cupcake papers. In a medium-sized bowl, lightly beat the eggs, add butter and sugar, then mix until light and fluffy.

2   Add buttermilk, flour, cocoa powder and vanilla, and stir to combine. Beat with an electric mixer for 2 minutes, until light and creamy. Add milk chocolate and stir through mixture.

3   Divide the mixture evenly between the cake papers. Bake for 18–20 minutes until risen and firm to touch. Allow to cool for a few minutes and then transfer to a wire rack. Allow to cool fully before icing.

Topping

1   Meanwhile, combine half the icing sugar and butter, mix with a wooden spoon, add remaining icing sugar, butter and food colouring and beat with the spoon until light and fluffy. Add icing to a piping bag and pipe onto cupcakes, then smooth over with spatula and top with flower decorations.

Makes 12

Jaffa Ganache Cupcakes

Preparation 12 mins **Cooking** 20 mins **Calories** 487 **Fat** 33g **Carbohydrate** 46g

3 eggs
1 cup butter, softened
1 cup caster sugar
½ cup milk
1½ cups self-raising flour, sifted
1 teaspoon vanilla extract
100g dark chocolate pieces
1 tablespoon cocoa powder
1 teaspoon orange essence

Topping
100g dark chocolate, grated
20g butter
⅓ cup cream, thickened
1 teaspoon orange essence
1 piece candied orange,
cut into slivers

1 Preheat the oven to 160°C. Line a 12-cupcake pan with cupcake papers. In a medium-sized bowl, lightly beat the eggs, add butter and sugar, then mix until light and fluffy.

2 Add milk, flour and vanilla, and stir to combine. Add remaining ingredients. Beat with an electric mixer for 2 minutes, until light and creamy.

3 Divide the mixture evenly between the cake papers. Bake for 18–20 minutes until risen and firm to touch. Allow to cool for a few minutes and then transfer to a wire rack. Allow to cool fully before icing.

Topping

1 Meanwhile, combine the chocolate and butter in a medium-sized saucepan over a medium heat. As the mixture begins to melt, reduce heat to low, stirring constantly, until melted. Remove from heat, add cream, orange essence, and stir. Rest for 10 minutes: the mixture will be firm and velvety in consistency. Once cool, put in a piping bag with a small plain nozzle.

2 Pipe topping onto cupcakes in a spiral and top with candied orange pieces.

Makes 12

Persian Chocolate Cupcakes

Preparation 12 mins **Cooking** 20 mins **Calories** 500 **Fat** 35g **Carbohydrate** 44g

3 eggs
1 cup butter, softened
1 cup caster sugar
½ cup milk
1½ cups self-raising flour, sifted
1 teaspoon vanilla extract
100g dark chocolate pieces
1 tablespoon cocoa powder

Topping
1½ cups icing sugar
½ cup butter, room temperature
2 teaspoons cocoa powder
small packet of persian fairy floss
1 tablespoon cocoa powder,
for dusting

1 Preheat the oven to 160°C. Line a 12-cupcake pan with cupcake papers. In a medium-sized bowl, lightly beat the eggs, add butter and sugar, then mix until light and fluffy.

2 Add milk, flour and vanilla, and stir to combine. Add remaining ingredients. Beat with an electric mixer for 2 minutes, until light and creamy.

3 Divide the mixture evenly between the cake papers. Bake for 18–20 minutes until risen and firm to touch. Allow to cool for a few minutes and then transfer to a wire rack. Allow to cool fully before icing.

Topping

1 Meanwhile, combine half the icing sugar and butter, mix with a wooden spoon, add remaining icing sugar, butter and cocoa powder and beat with the spoon until light and fluffy.

2 Add icing to a piping bag with a small nozzle and pipe onto cupcakes in a spiral. Top with persian fairy floss and a dusting of cocoa.

Makes 12

Vanilla Choc Cupcakes

Preparation 12 mins **Cooking** 20 mins **Calories** 461 **Fat** 30g **Carbohydrate** 45g

3 eggs
1 cup butter, softened
1 cup caster sugar
½ cup vanilla-flavoured yoghurt
1½ cups self-raising flour, sifted
1 tablespoon vanilla extract
100g dark chocolate pieces
1 tablespoon cocoa

Topping
100g dark chocolate pieces
20g butter
⅓ cup cream, thickened
silver balls (available from cake decoration stores)

1 Preheat the oven to 160°C. Line a 12-cupcake pan with cupcake papers. In a medium-sized bowl, lightly beat the eggs, add butter and sugar, then mix until light and fluffy.

2 Add milk, flour and vanilla, and stir to combine. Add remaining ingredients. Beat with an electric mixer for 2 minutes, until light and creamy.

3 Divide the mixture evenly between the cake papers. Bake for 18–20 minutes until risen and firm to touch. Allow to cool for a few minutes, and then transfer to a wire rack. Allow to cool fully before icing.

Topping

1 Meanwhile, combine the chocolate and butter in a medium-sized saucepan over a medium heat. As the mixture begins to melt, reduce heat to low, stirring constantly, until melted. Remove from heat, add cream, and stir. Rest for 10 minutes: the mixture will be firm and velvety in consistency. Use a fork to apply icing to each cupcake, and add silver balls to finish.

Makes 12

Hazel Choc Cupcakes

Preparation 12 mins **Cooking** 20 mins **Calories** 662 **Fat** 49g **Carbohydrate** 52g

3 eggs
1 cup butter, softened
1 cup caster sugar
½ cup milk
1½ cups self-raising flour, sifted
1 teaspoon vanilla extract
100g dark chocolate pieces
1 tablespoon cocoa powder

Topping
100g dark chocolate pieces
1 tablespoon butter
⅓ cup cream, thickened
½ cup butter, room temperature
1 cup icing sugar
100g hazelnuts

1 Preheat the oven to 160°C. Line a 12-cupcake pan with cupcake papers. In a medium-sized bowl, lightly beat the eggs, add butter and sugar, then mix until light and fluffy.

2 Add milk, flour and vanilla, and stir to combine. Add remaining ingredients. Beat with an electric mixer for 2 minutes, until light and creamy.

3 Divide the mixture evenly between the cake papers. Bake for 18–20 minutes until risen and firm to touch. Allow to cool for a few minutes and then transfer to a wire rack. Allow to cool fully before icing.

Topping

1 Meanwhile, combine the chocolate and 1 tablespoon of butter in a medium-sized saucepan over a medium heat. As the mixture begins to melt, add cream slowly, then reduce heat to low, stirring constantly, until mixture thickens. Remove from heat and cool.

2 Combine butter and icing sugar, and mix with wooden spoon. Beat with the spoon until light and fluffy. Add melted chocolate and ½ of the hazelnuts, combine, and then spoon onto cupcakes. Top with the remaining nuts.

Makes 12

Chilli Choc Cupcakes

Preparation 12 mins **Cooking** 20 mins **Calories** 487 **Fat** 33g **Carbohydrate** 46g

2 small fresh chillies or 1 teaspoon
dry red chilli flakes
3 eggs
1 cup butter, softened
1 cup caster sugar
½ cup milk
1½ cups self-raising flour, sifted
1 teaspoon vanilla extract
100g dark chocolate pieces
1 tablespoon cocoa powder

Topping
100g dark chocolate, chopped
20g butter
⅓ cup cream, thickened
remaining chilli-infused water
chillies for decoration

1 Preheat the oven to 160°C. Line a 12-cupcake pan with cupcake papers. Slice chillies down the centre, and remove seeds – place the chillies in a cup with ¼ cup of hot water to soak for 10 minutes. In a medium-sized bowl, lightly beat the eggs, add butter and sugar, then mix until light and fluffy.

2 Add milk, flour and vanilla, and stir to combine. Add ½ cup dark chocolate, cocoa powder and ½ the chilli-infused water and combine. Beat with an electric mixer for 2 minutes, until light and creamy.

3 Divide the mixture evenly between the cake papers. Bake for 18–20 minutes until risen and firm to touch. Allow to cool for a few minutes and then transfer to a wire rack. Allow to cool fully before icing.

Topping

1 Meanwhile, combine the chocolate and butter in a medium-sized saucepan over a medium heat. As the mixture begins to melt, reduce heat to low, stirring constantly, until melted. Remove from heat, add cream, remaining chilli water and stir. Rest for 10 minutes: the mixture will be firm and velvety in consistency. Put in a piping bag with a small plain nozzle and pipe onto cakes. Top with fresh small chillies.

Makes 12

Triple Choc Cupcakes

Preparation 12 mins **Cooking** 20 mins **Calories** 480 **Fat** 32g **Carbohydrate** 45g

3 eggs
1 cup butter, softened
1 cup caster sugar
½ cup milk
1½ cups self-raising flour, sifted
100g dark chocolate pieces
1 tablespoon cocoa powder

Topping
100g dark chocolate, chopped
20g butter
⅓ cup cream, thickened
2 tablespoons cocoa powder
1 teaspoon icing sugar

1 Preheat the oven to 160°C. Line a 12-cupcake pan with cupcake papers. In a medium-sized bowl, lightly beat the eggs, add butter and sugar, then mix until light and fluffy.

2 Add milk and flour, and stir to combine. Add ½ cup dark chocolate and cocoa powder, and stir through mixture. Beat with an electric mixer for 2 minutes, until light and creamy.

3 Divide the mixture evenly between the cupcake papers. Bake for 18–20 minutes until risen and firm to touch. Allow to cool for a few minutes and then transfer to a wire rack. Allow to cool fully before icing.

Topping

1 Meanwhile, combine the chocolate and butter in a medium-sized saucepan over a medium heat. As the mixture begins to melt, reduce heat to low, stirring constantly, until melted. Remove from heat, add cream, cocoa powder and icing sugar, and stir to combine. Rest for 10 minutes: the mixture will be firm and velvety in consistency. Use the back of a spoon to apply icing to cupcake.

Makes 12

Choc Chip Cupcakes

Preparation 12 mins **Cooking** 20 mins **Calories** 644 **Fat** 46g **Carbohydrate** 56g

3 eggs
1 cup butter, softened
1 cup caster sugar
½ cup milk
1½ cups self-raising flour, sifted
1 teaspoon vanilla extract
120g milk chocolate drops
1 tablespoon cocoa powder

Topping
200g milk chocolate, grated
⅓ cup cream, thickened
½ cup butter
1½ cups icing sugar
1 teaspoon vanilla extract
½ cup milk chocolate drops
½ cup small choc drops

1 Preheat the oven to 160°C. Line a 12-cupcake pan with cupcake papers. In a medium-sized bowl, lightly beat the eggs, add butter and sugar, then mix until light and fluffy.

2 Beat with an electric mixer for 2 minutes, until light and creamy. Add milk, flour and vanilla, and stir to combine. Add ½ cup milk chocolate and cocoa powder, and stir through mixture.

3 Divide the mixture evenly between the cupcake papers. Bake for 18–20 minutes until risen and firm to touch. Allow to cool for a few minutes and then transfer to a wire rack. Allow to cool fully before icing.

Topping

1 Meanwhile, combine the chocolate and cream in a medium-sized saucepan over a medium heat. As the mixture begins to melt, reduce heat to low, stirring constantly, until melted. Remove from heat, cool.

2 Combine butter, icing sugar and vanilla extract, stir until light and fluffy. Add melted chocolate mixture, stir in chocolate drops and spoon onto cupcakes. Sprinkle with small chocolate drops.

Makes 12

Chocolate Honeycomb Cupcakes

Preparation 12 mins **Cooking** 20 mins **Calories** 716 **Fat** 51g **Carbohydrate** 62g

3 eggs
1 cup butter, softened
1 cup caster sugar
½ cup buttermilk
1½ cups self-raising flour, sifted
1 teaspoon vanilla extract

Topping
½ cup chocolate drops
½ cup butter, room temperature
⅓ cup cream, thickened
1½ cups icing sugar
1 teaspoon vanilla extract
½ cup pre-made honeycomb pieces

1 Preheat the oven to 160°C. Line a 12-cupcake pan with cupcake papers. In a medium-sized bowl, lightly beat the eggs, add butter and sugar, then mix until light and fluffy.

2 Add buttermilk, flour and vanilla, and stir to combine. Beat with an electric mixer for 2 minutes, until light and creamy.

3 Divide the mixture evenly between the cupcake papers. Bake for 18–20 minutes until risen and firm to touch. Allow to cool for a few minutes and then transfer to a wire rack. Allow to cool fully before icing.

Topping

1 Meanwhile, combine the chocolate and half of the butter in a medium-sized saucepan over a medium heat. As the mixture begins to melt, reduce heat to low, stirring constantly, until melted. Remove from heat, add cream, and stir. Rest for 10 minutes, the mixture will be firm and velvety in consistency.

2 Combine remaining butter, icing sugar and vanilla extract, and stir until light and fluffy. Add melted chocolate mixture, and stir to combine. Apply icing to each cupcake with a knife. Top each cupcake with a cluster of crumbled honeycomb.

Makes 12

Chocky Road Cupcakes

Preparation 12 mins   **Cooking** 20 mins   **Calories** 707   **Fat** 50g   **Carbohydrate** 64g

3 eggs
1 cup butter, softened
1 cup caster sugar
½ cup milk
1½ cups self-raising flour, sifted
1 teaspoon vanilla extract
1 tablespoon cocoa powder

Topping
½ cup milk chocolate drops
½ cup butter, room temperature
⅓ cup cream, thickened
1½ cups icing sugar
1 teaspoon vanilla extract
¼ cup glacé cherries, chopped
⅓ cup almonds, chopped
⅓ cup marshmallows, chopped

1 Preheat the oven to 160°C. Line a 12-cupcake pan with cupcake papers. In a medium-sized bowl, lightly beat the eggs, add butter and sugar, then mix until light and fluffy.

2 Add milk, flour, vanilla and cocoa powder, and stir to combine. Beat with an electric mixer for 2 minutes, until light and creamy.

3 Divide the mixture evenly between the cupcake papers. Bake for 18–20 minutes until risen and firm to touch. Allow to cool for a few minutes and then transfer to a wire rack. Allow to cool fully before icing.

Topping

1 Meanwhile, combine the chocolate and half of the butter in a medium-sized saucepan over a medium heat. As the mixture begins to melt, reduce heat to low, stirring constantly, until melted. Remove from heat, add cream, and stir. Rest for 10 minutes: the mixture will be firm and velvety in consistency.

2 Combine remaining butter, icing sugar and vanilla extract, and stir until light and fluffy. Add melted chocolate mixture and stir to combine. Ice the top of each cupcake and decorate with pieces of cherry, almonds and marshmallows.

Makes 12

Cherry Top Cupcakes

Preparation 12 mins **Cooking** 20 mins **Calories** 743 **Fat** 51g **Carbohydrate** 68g

3 eggs
1 cup butter, softened
1 cup caster sugar
½ cup milk
1½ cups self-raising flour, sifted
1 teaspoon vanilla extract
1 tablespoon cocoa powder

Topping
1 cup dark chocolate drops
20g butter, room temperature
⅓ cup cream, thickened
6 glacé cherries, halved

1 Preheat the oven to 160°C. Line a 12-cupcake pan with cupcake papers. In a medium-sized bowl, lightly beat the eggs, add butter and sugar, then mix until light and fluffy.

2 Add milk, flour, vanilla and cocoa powder, and stir to combine. Beat with an electric mixer for 2 minutes, until light and creamy.

3 Divide the mixture evenly between the cupcake cases. Bake for 18–20 minutes until risen and firm to touch. Allow to cool for a few minutes and then transfer to a wire rack. Allow to cool fully before icing.

Topping

1 Meanwhile, combine the chocolate and butter in a medium-sized saucepan over a medium heat. As the mixture begins to melt, reduce heat to low, stirring constantly, until melted. Remove from heat, add cream, and stir. Rest for 10 minutes: the mixture will be firm and velvety in consistency.

2 Spoon into a piping bag with a broad nozzle, and pipe onto cupcakes in a spiral. Top with cherry pieces.

Makes 12

Almond Choc Cupcakes

Preparation 12 mins **Cooking** 45 mins **Calories** 764 **Fat** 56g **Carbohydrate** 61g

3 eggs
1 cup butter, softened
1 cup caster sugar
½ cup milk
1½ cups self-raising flour, sifted
1 teaspoon vanilla extract
1 tablespoon cocoa powder

Topping
½ cup caster sugar, for toffee
100g dark chocolate
20g butter
⅓ cup cream, thickened
1 cup icing sugar
1 tablespoon cocoa powder
½ cup dark chocolate
100g almond flakes

1 Preheat the oven to 160°C. Line a 12-cupcake pan with cupcake papers. In a medium-sized bowl, lightly beat the eggs, add butter and sugar, then mix until light and fluffy.

2 Add milk, flour, vanilla and cocoa powder, and stir to combine. Beat with an electric mixer for 2 minutes, until light and creamy.

3 Divide the mixture evenly between the cupcake papers. Bake for 18–20 minutes until risen and firm to touch. Allow to cool for a few minutes and then transfer to a wire rack. Allow to cool fully before icing.

Toffee

1 Place ½ cup caster sugar evenly on a greaseproof paper-lined baking tray, and bake in oven on 200°C for approximately 25 minutes until toffee consistency forms. Cool until hardened.

Topping

1 Combine the chocolate and butter in a medium-sized saucepan over a medium heat. As the mixture begins to melt, reduce heat to low, stirring constantly, until melted. Remove from heat, add cream, and stir. Rest for 10 minutes: the mixture will be firm and velvety in consistency.

2 Combine the icing sugar and cocoa powder, mix with wooden spoon until mixed together, beat with spoon until light and fluffy. Add the chocolate mixture to the butter cream and mix with a wooden spoon until light and fluffy. Ice the cakes. Decorate with almond and broken toffee pieces.

Makes 12

Cherry Choc Cupcakes

Preparation 12 mins **Cooking** 20 mins **Calories** 701 **Fat** 50g **Carbohydrate** 62g

3 eggs
1 cup butter, softened
1 cup caster sugar
½ cup milk
1 tablespoon kirsch liqueur
1½ cups self-raising flour, sifted
200g white chocolate, chopped

Topping

100g white chocolate, chopped
1 tablespoon butter
⅓ cup cream, thickened
1 tablespoon cherry liqueur
⅔ cup icing sugar
½ cup butter, room temperature
200g glacé cherries, chopped

1. Preheat the oven to 160°C. Line a 12-cupcake pan with cupcake papers. In a medium-sized bowl, lightly beat the eggs, add butter and sugar, then mix until light and fluffy.

2. Add milk, liqueur and flour, and stir to combine. Beat with an electric mixer for 2 minutes, until light and creamy. Add white chocolate, and stir through mixture.

3. Divide the mixture evenly between the cake papers. Bake for 18–20 minutes until risen and firm to touch. Allow to cool for a few minutes and then transfer to a wire rack. Allow to cool fully before icing.

Topping

1. Meanwhile, combine the chocolate and tablespoon of butter in a medium-sized saucepan over a medium heat. As the mixture begins to melt, add cream and liqueur slowly, then reduce heat to low, stirring constantly until mixture thickens. Remove from heat and cool.

2. Combine butter and icing sugar, and mix with a wooden spoon. Beat with the spoon until light and fluffy. Add melted chocolate and glacé cherries, stir until combined, and then spoon onto cupcakes.

Makes 12

Fruit
Cupcakes

Fresh fruits, fruit juices and fruit flavourings add texture and variety to your cupcake creations, making the perfect treat for the lunch box or after school, and a great mid-afternoon pick-me-up with a hot drink.

Triple Berry Cupcakes

Preparation 12 mins **Cooking** 20 mins **Calories** 325 **Fat** 20g **Carbohydrate** 34g

3 eggs
½ cup butter, softened
1 cup caster sugar
½ cup milk
2 tablespoons framboise liqueur
1½ cups self-raising flour, sifted

Topping
½ cup icing sugar
2 tablespoons water
½ punnet strawberries
½ punnet blueberries
½ punnet blackberries

1 Preheat the oven to 160°C. Line a 12-cupcake pan with cupcake papers. In a medium-sized bowl, lightly beat the eggs, add butter and sugar, then mix until light and fluffy.

2 Add milk, liqueur and flour, and stir to combine. Beat with an electric mixer for 2 minutes, until light and creamy.

3 Divide the mixture evenly between the cake papers. Bake for 18–20 minutes until risen and firm to touch. Allow to cool for a few minutes and then transfer to a wire rack. Allow to cool fully before icing.

Topping

1 Meanwhile, combine icing sugar and water in a small bowl. Spoon a teaspoon of icing in the centre of each cupcake. Decorate with a cluster of fresh berries.

Makes 12

Passion Yoghurt Cupcakes

Preparation 12 mins **Cooking** 20 mins **Calories** 420 **Fat** 24g **Carbohydrate** 48g

3 eggs
½ cup butter, softened
1 cup caster sugar
½ cup plain yoghurt
1½ cups self-raising flour, sifted
1 teaspoon vanilla extract
the pulp of 2 passionfruit

Topping
1 cup icing sugar
½ cup of greek-style yoghurt
the pulp of 1 passionfruit

1 Preheat the oven to 160°C. Line a 12 cupcake pan with cupcake papers. In a medium-sized bowl, lightly beat the eggs, add butter and sugar, then mix until light and fluffy.

2 Add yoghurt, flour and vanilla, and stir to combine. Beat with an electric mixer for 2 minutes, until light and creamy. Fold passionfruit pulp through mixture.

3 Divide the mixture evenly between the cake papers. Bake for 18–20 minutes until risen and firm to touch. Allow to cool for a few minutes and then transfer to a wire rack. Allow to cool fully before icing.

Topping

1 Meanwhile, combine icing sugar and yoghurt in a medium-sized bowl and mix with a wooden spoon. Add passionfruit pulp, mix to combine and spread topping on cupcakes.

Makes 12

Black Forest Cupcakes

Preparation 12 mins **Cooking** 20 mins **Calories** 346 **Fat** 22g **Carbohydrate** 33g

3 eggs
½ cup butter, softened
1 cup caster sugar
½ cup milk
1½ cups self-raising flour, sifted
1 tablespoon kirsch liqueur
¼ cup cocoa powder

Topping
100g fresh cream
12 fresh cherries
¼ cup chocolate, shaved

1 Preheat the oven to 160°C. Line a 12-cupcake pan with cupcake papers. In a medium-sized bowl, lightly beat the eggs, add butter and sugar, then mix until light and fluffy.

2 Add milk, flour and cocoa powder, and stir to combine. Beat with an electric mixer for 2 minutes, until light and creamy, then fold through kirsch liqueur.

3 Divide the mixture evenly between the cake papers. Bake for 18–20 minutes until risen and firm to touch. Allow to cool for a few minutes and then transfer to a wire rack. Allow to cool fully before icing.

Topping

1 Meanwhile, whip cream until stiff peaks form, then top each cake with a dollop of cream, a sprinkle of chocolate shavings and a fresh cherry.

Makes 12

Poppy Lime Cupcakes

Preparation 12 mins **Cooking** 20 mins **Calories** 489 **Fat** 35g **Carbohydrate** 42g

3 eggs
½ cup butter, softened
1 cup caster sugar
½ cup greek-style yoghurt
1½ cups self-raising flour, sifted
zest of 2 limes
juice of 1 lime
1 teaspoon poppy seeds

Topping
1½ cups icing sugar
½ cup butter, room temperature
juice of 1 lime
½ teaspoon poppy seeds
zest of 1 lime
50g candied lime,
cut into thin slivers

1. Preheat the oven to 160°C. Line a 12-cupcake pan with cupcake papers. In a medium-sized bowl, lightly beat the eggs, add butter and sugar, then mix until light and fluffy.
2. Add yoghurt and flour, and stir to combine. Beat with an electric mixer for 2 minutes, until light and creamy. Add lime zest, lime juice and poppy seeds, and mix through with a wooden spoon.
3. Divide the mixture evenly between the cake cases. Bake for 18–20 minutes until risen and firm to touch. Allow to cool for a few minutes and then transfer to a wire rack. Allow to cool fully before icing.

Topping
1. Meanwhile, combine the topping ingredients, mix with a wooden spoon, and spoon onto cakes. Top with candied lime pieces.

Makes 12

Apple and Cinnamon Cupcakes

Preparation 12 mins **Cooking** 20 mins **Calories** 486 **Fat** 35g **Carbohydrate** 43g

½ apple, peeled and chopped into small pieces
juice of 1 lemon
1 tablespoon cinnamon
3 eggs
½ cup butter, softened
1 cup caster sugar
½ cup milk
1½ cups self-raising flour, sifted

Topping
1½ cups icing sugar
½ cup butter, room temperature
1 tablespoon cinnamon sugar

1   Preheat the oven to 160°C. Line a 12-cupcake pan with cupcake papers. In a small bowl, coat the apple pieces with lemon juice and sprinkle with cinnamon. In a medium-sized bowl, lightly beat the eggs, add butter and sugar, then mix until light and fluffy.

2   Add milk and flour, and stir to combine. Beat with an electric mixer for 2 minutes, until light and creamy. Add spiced apple and stir through mixture.

3   Divide the mixture evenly between the cake papers. Bake for 18–20 minutes until risen and firm to touch. Allow to cool for a few minutes and then transfer to a wire rack. Allow to cool fully before icing.

Topping

1   Meanwhile, combine half the icing sugar and butter, mix with a wooden spoon, add remaining icing sugar and butter and beat with the spoon until light and fluffy. Spoon topping onto cupcakes and sprinkle cinnamon sugar on top.

Makes 12

Orange Poppy Cupcakes

Preparation 12 mins **Cooking** 20 mins **Calories** 494 **Fat** 35g **Carbohydrate** 43g

3 eggs
½ cup butter, softened
1 cup caster sugar
½ cup buttermilk
1½ cups self-raising flour, sifted
zest of 1 orange
juice of ½ orange
1 teaspoon poppy seeds

Topping
1½ cups icing sugar
½ cup butter, room temperature
juice of ½ orange
½ teaspoon poppy seeds
zest of 1 orange
candied orange pieces,
cut into thin slivers

1 Preheat the oven to 160°C. Line a 12-cupcake pan with cupcake papers. In a medium-sized bowl, lightly beat the eggs, add butter and sugar, then mix until light and fluffy.

2 Add buttermilk and flour, and stir to combine. Beat with an electric mixer for 2 minutes, until light and creamy. Add orange zest, orange juice and poppy seeds, and mix through with a wooden spoon.

3 Divide the mixture evenly between the cake cases. Bake for 18–20 minutes until risen and firm to touch. Allow to cool for a few minutes and then transfer to a wire rack. Allow to cool fully before icing.

Topping

1 Meanwhile, combine topping ingredients, and mix with a wooden spoon. Spoon onto cakes. Top with candied orange pieces.

Makes 12

Blue Bell Cupcakes

Preparation 12 mins **Cooking** 20 mins **Calories** 323 **Fat** 18g **Carbohydrate** 37g

3 eggs
½ cup butter, softened
1 cup caster sugar
½ cup milk
1½ cups self-raising flour, sifted
1 teaspoon vanilla extract
½ punnet blueberries, chopped in half

Topping
1 cup icing sugar
2 tablespoons of blueberries, mashed
½ punnet blueberries

1 Preheat the oven to 160°C. Line a 12-cupcake pan with cupcake papers. In a medium-sized bowl, lightly beat the eggs, add butter and sugar, then mix until light and fluffy.

2 Add milk, flour and vanilla, and stir to combine. Beat with an electric mixer for 2 minutes, until light and creamy. Add blueberries and stir through the mixture.

3 Divide the mixture evenly between the cake papers. Bake for 18–20 minutes until risen and firm to touch. Allow to cool for a few minutes and then transfer to a wire rack. Allow to cool fully before icing.

Topping

1 Meanwhile, combine icing sugar and mashed berries in a medium-sized bowl and mix with wooden spoon. Use a spatula to apply icing to each cupcake and top with a blueberry.

Makes 12

Banana Nut Cupcakes

Preparation 12 mins **Cooking** 20 mins **Calories** 529 **Fat** 38g **Carbohydrate** 44g

3 eggs
½ cup butter, softened
1 cup caster sugar
½ cup milk
1½ cups self-raising flour, sifted
1 teaspoon smooth peanut butter
1 sugar banana, mashed

Topping
½ cup caster sugar, for toffee
1½ cups icing sugar
½ cup butter, room temperature
2 tablespoons crunchy unsalted peanut butter
1 tablespoon golden syrup

1 Preheat the oven to 160°C. Line a 12-cupcake pan with cupcake papers. In a medium-sized bowl, lightly beat the eggs, add butter and sugar, then mix until light and fluffy.

2 Add milk, flour, peanut butter and banana, and stir to combine. Beat with an electric mixer for 2 minutes, until light and creamy. Add banana and stir through mix.

3 Divide the mixture evenly between the cake papers. Bake for 18–20 minutes until risen and firm to touch. Allow to cool for a few minutes and then transfer to a wire rack. Allow to cool fully before icing.

Toffee

1 Place ½ cup caster sugar evenly on a greaseproof paper-lined baking tray, and bake in oven on 200°C for approximately 25 minutes until toffee consistency forms. Cool until hardened.

Topping

1 Meanwhile, combine half the icing sugar, butter and peanut butter, and mix with a wooden spoon, then add remaining icing sugar, butter and peanut butter and beat with the spoon until light and fluffy. Use the back of a spoon to ice cakes. Drizzle golden syrup onto cakes and top with toffee pieces.

Makes 12

Peachy Cupcakes

Preparation 12 mins **Cooking** 20 mins **Calories** 497 **Fat** 35g **Carbohydrate** 45g

3 eggs
½ cup butter, softened
1 cup caster sugar
½ cup milk
1½ cups self-raising flour, sifted
2 tablespoons peach liqueur

Topping
1½ cups icing sugar
½ cup butter, room temperature
1 teaspoon peach essence
1 drop orange food colouring
1 drop red food colouring
peach-coloured sugar flowers
(available from cake
decoration stores)

1 Preheat the oven to 160°C. Line a 12-cupcake pan with cupcake papers. In a medium-sized bowl, lightly beat the eggs, add butter and sugar, then mix until light and fluffy.

2 Add milk, flour and peach liqueur, stir to combine. Beat with an electric mixer for 2 minutes, until light and creamy.

3 Divide the mixture evenly between the cake cases. Bake for 18–20 minutes until risen and firm to touch. Allow to cool for a few minutes and then transfer to a wire rack. Allow to cool fully before icing.

Topping

1 Meanwhile, combine all topping ingredients except sugar flower into a small bowl, and mix with a wooden spoon until well combined, then beat with a whisk until light and fluffy. Spoon mixture into a piping bag and pipe dots onto all cupcakes. Top each dot of icing with flowers.

Makes 12

Strawberry Surprise Cupcakes

Preparation 12 mins **Cooking** 20 mins **Calories** 510 **Fat** 35g **Carbohydrate** 50g

3 eggs
½ cup butter, softened
1 cup caster sugar
½ cup milk
1½ cups self-raising flour, sifted
2 tablespoons strawberry liqueur

Topping
1½ cups icing sugar
½ cup butter, room temperature
3 strawberries, quartered
strawberry-coloured flowers
(available from cake
decoration stores)

1 Preheat the oven to 160°C. Line a 12-cupcake pan, with cupcake papers. In a medium-sized bowl, lightly beat the eggs, add butter and sugar, then mix until light and fluffy.

2 Add milk, flour and liqueur, and stir to combine. Beat with an electric mixer for 2 minutes, until light and creamy.

3 Divide the mixture evenly between the cake papers. Bake for 18–20 minutes until risen and firm to touch. Allow to cool for a few minutes and then transfer to a wire rack. Allow to cool fully before icing.

Topping

1 Meanwhile, combine icing sugar and butter into a small bowl, mix with a wooden spoon until well combined, then beat with a whisk until light and fluffy. Spoon mixture into a piping bag with a medium-sized star-shaped nozzle, and set aside.

2 With a sharp knife, slash the top of each cupcake and push a piece of strawberry into the centre. Pip icing onto each cupcake and decorate with the red sugar flowers. Serve immediately.

Makes 12

Jaffa Choc Cupcakes

Preparation 12 mins **Cooking** 20 mins **Calories** 509 **Fat** 36g **Carbohydrate** 45g

3 eggs
½ cup butter, softened
1 cup caster sugar
½ cup milk
1½ cups self-raising flour, sifted
1 teaspoon cocoa powder
1 teaspoon vanilla extract
juice of 1 orange
zest of 1 orange
¼ cup chocolate chips or flakes

Topping
2 cups icing sugar
½ cup butter, room temperature
⅓ cup orange juice
¼ cup chocolate, finely chopped

1 Preheat the oven to 160°C. Line a 12-cupcake pan with cupcake papers. In a medium-sized bowl, lightly beat the eggs, add butter and sugar, then mix until light and fluffy.

2 Add milk, flour, cocoa powder and vanilla, and stir to combine. Beat with an electric mixer for 2 minutes, until light and creamy. Add juice, zest and chocolate chips.

3 Divide the mixture evenly between the cake papers. Bake for 18–20 minutes until risen and firm to touch. Allow to cool for a few minutes and then transfer to a wire rack. Allow to cool fully before icing.

Topping

1 Meanwhile, combine half the topping ingredients except the chocolate, mix with a wooden spoon, add remaining ingredients and beat with the spoon until light and fluffy. Add chocolate and stir through. Spoon onto cakes.

Makes 12

Lime and Pistachio Cupcakes

Preparation 12 mins **Cooking** 20 mins **Calories** 504 **Fat** 33g **Carbohydrate** 47g

3 eggs
½ cup butter, softened
1 cup caster sugar
½ cup milk
2 cups self-raising flour, sifted
1 teaspoon vanilla extract
½ cup pistachio nuts
juice of ½ a lime
zest of 1 lime

Topping
1½ cups icing sugar
½ cup butter, room temperature
zest of 1 lime
½ cup pistachio nuts

1 Preheat the oven to 160°C. Line a 12-cupcake pan with cupcake papers. In a medium-sized bowl, lightly beat the eggs, add butter and sugar, then mix until light and fluffy.

2 Add milk, flour and vanilla, and stir to combine. Beat with an electric mixer for 2 minutes, until light and creamy. Add pistachio nuts, lime juice and zest, and combine.

3 Divide the mixture evenly between the cake papers. Bake for 18–20 minutes until risen and firm to touch. Allow to cool for a few minutes and then transfer to a wire rack. Allow to cool fully before icing.

Topping

1 Meanwhile, combine icing sugar and butter, mix with a wooden spoon and beat until light and fluffy. Add lime zest and pistachio nuts and mix through. Spoon onto cupcakes in large, loose dollops.

Makes 12

Ginger Lime Cupcakes

Preparation 12 mins **Cooking** 20 mins **Calories** 326 **Fat** 18g **Carbohydrate** 38g

3 eggs
½ cup butter, softened
1 cup caster sugar
½ cup buttermilk
2 cups self-raising flour, sifted
½ cup crystallised ginger, finely chopped
juice of ½ a lime
zest of 1 lime
½ cup icing sugar
50g crystallised ginger

1 Preheat the oven to 160°C. Line a 12-cupcake pan with cupcake papers. In a medium-sized bowl, lightly beat the eggs, add butter and sugar, then mix until light and fluffy.

2 Add buttermilk and flour, and stir to combine. Beat with an electric mixer for 2 minutes, until light and creamy. Add crystallised ginger, lime juice and zest, and mix through until combined.

3 Divide the mixture evenly between the cake papers. Bake for 18–20 minutes until risen and firm to touch. Allow to cool for a few minutes and then transfer to a wire rack.

4 Top with slices of crystallised ginger and dust with icing sugar.

Makes 12

Orange Choc Swirl Cupcakes

Preparation 12 mins **Cooking** 20 mins **Calories** 305 **Fat** 19g **Carbohydrate** 31g

3 eggs
½ cup butter, softened
1 cup caster sugar
½ cup milk
2 cups self-raising flour, sifted
¼ cup cocoa powder
juice of ½ an orange
zest of ½ an orange

1 Preheat the oven to 160°C. Line a 12-cupcake pan with cupcake papers. In a medium-sized bowl, lightly beat the eggs, add butter and sugar, then mix until light and fluffy.

2 Add milk and flour, and stir to combine. Beat with an electric mixer for 2 minutes, until light and creamy. Divide mixture into two bowls. Into bowl one, add orange juice and zest. Into bowl two, add cocoa. Add ½ mixture of each into each cake paper and gently stir with a skewer to get a marble effect.

3 Bake for 18–20 minutes until risen and firm to touch. Allow to cool for a few minutes and then transfer to a wire rack.

Makes 12

Novelties and Nuts

A chapter full of playful toppings and rich, dense cakes: almond meal and nut toppings combine to create moist and delicious treats. Let your imagination take you away.

Green and Gold Cupcakes

Preparation 12 mins **Cooking** 20 mins **Calories** 329 **Fat** 18g **Carbohydrate** 38g

3 eggs
½ cup butter, softened
1 cup caster sugar
½ cup milk
1½ cups self-raising flour, sifted
1 teaspoon vanilla extract
½ teaspoon yellow food colouring
zest of 1 lemon

Topping
1½ cups icing sugar
½ cup butter, room temperature
2 drops green food colouring
12 novelty candles and
Australian flags

1 Preheat the oven to 160°C. Line a 12-cupcake pan with cupcake papers. In a medium-sized bowl, lightly beat the eggs, add butter and sugar, then mix until light and fluffy.

2 Add milk, flour, vanilla, yellow food colouring and zest and stir to combine. Beat with an electric mixer for 2 minutes, until light and creamy.

3 Divide the mixture evenly between the cake papers. Bake for 18–20 minutes until risen and firm to touch. Allow to cool for a few minutes and then transfer to a wire rack. Allow to cool fully before icing.

Topping

1 Meanwhile, combine all the topping ingredients, and mix with a wooden spoon until well combined. Using the back of a teaspoon, apply icing to each cupcake. Top each cupcake with a novelty candle and flag.

Makes 12

Easter Choc Cupcakes

Preparation 12 mins **Cooking** 20 mins **Calories** 596 **Fat** 42g **Carbohydrate** 52g

3 eggs
½ cup butter, softened
1 cup caster sugar
½ cup milk
1½ cups self-raising flour, sifted
1 teaspoon vanilla extract
200g dark chocolate pieces
1 tablespoon cocoa powder

Topping
100g dark chocolate
1 tablespoon butter
⅓ cup cream, thickened
½ cup butter, room temperature
1 cup icing sugar
36 small easter eggs

1 Preheat the oven to 160°C. Line a 12-cupcake pan with cupcake papers. In a medium-sized bowl, lightly beat the eggs, add butter and sugar, then mix until light and fluffy.

2 Add milk, flour and vanilla, and stir to combine. Add remaining ingredients. Beat with an electric mixer for 2 minutes, until light and creamy.

3 Divide the mixture evenly between the cake papers. Bake for 18–20 minutes until risen and firm to touch. Allow to cool for a few minutes and then transfer to a wire rack. Allow to cool fully before icing.

Topping

1 Meanwhile, combine the chocolate and tablespoon of butter in a medium-sized saucepan over a medium heat. As the mixture begins to melt, add cream slowly, then reduce heat to low, stirring constantly, until mixture thickens. Remove from heat and cool.

2 Combine butter and icing sugar, mix with a wooden spoon, then beat with the spoon until light and fluffy. Add melted chocolate and combine. Spoon onto cupcakes and place 3 easter eggs on top of each cupcake.

Makes 12

Lamington Top Cupcakes

Preparation 12 mins **Cooking** 20 mins **Calories** 626 **Fat** 46g **Carbohydrate** 51g

3 eggs
½ cup butter, softened
1 cup caster sugar
½ cup milk
1½ cups self-raising flour, sifted
1 teaspoon vanilla extract
1 tablespoon cocoa powder

Topping
100g dark chocolate
1 tablespoon butter
⅓ cup cream, thickened
1 cup icing sugar
½ cup butter, room temperature
200g shredded coconut

1 Preheat the oven to 160°C. Line a 12-cupcake pan with cupcake papers. In a medium-sized bowl, lightly beat the eggs, add butter and sugar, then mix until light and fluffy.

2 Add milk, flour and vanilla, and stir to combine. Add remaining ingredients. Beat with an electric mixer for 2 minutes, until light and creamy.

3 Divide the mixture evenly between the cake papers. Bake for 18–20 minutes until risen and firm to touch. Allow to cool for a few minutes and then transfer to a wire rack. Allow to cool fully before icing.

Topping

1 Meanwhile, combine the chocolate and tablespoon of butter in a medium-sized saucepan over a medium heat. As the mixture begins to melt, add cream slowly, then reduce heat to low, stirring constantly, until mixture thickens. Remove from heat and cool.

2 Combine butter and icing sugar, mix with a wooden spoon, then beat with the spoon until light and fluffy. Add melted chocolate and combine, and spoon icing onto cupcakes. Place coconut onto a small plate and roll each cupcake on it to achieve desired effect.

Makes 12

Vanilla Rudolph Cupcakes

Preparation 12 mins **Cooking** 20 mins **Calories** 713 **Fat** 81g **Carbohydrate** 61g

3 eggs
½ cup butter, softened
1 cup caster sugar
½ cup milk
1½ cups self-raising flour, sifted
2 teaspoons vanilla extract

Topping
100g dark chocolate
1 tablespoon butter
⅓ cup cream, thickened
novelty reindeers (available from specialist cake decoration stores)

1 Preheat the oven to 160°C. Line a 12-cupcake pan with cupcake papers. In a medium-sized bowl, lightly beat the eggs, add butter and sugar, then mix until light and fluffy.

2 Add milk, flour and vanilla, and stir to combine. Beat with an electric mixer for 2 minutes, until light and creamy.

3 Divide the mixture evenly between the cake papers. Bake for 18–20 minutes until risen and firm to touch. Allow to cool for a few minutes and then transfer to a wire rack. Allow to cool fully before icing.

Topping

1 Meanwhile, combine the chocolate and butter in a medium-sized saucepan over a medium heat. As the mixture begins to melt, reduce heat to low, and add cream slowly, stirring constantly until the mixture thickens. Remove from heat and cool. Decorate the top of each cake with a novelty reindeer.

Makes 12

Toffee Meringue Crunch Cupcakes

Preparation 12 mins **Cooking** 30 mins **Calories** 530 **Fat** 27g **Carbohydrate** 69g

3 eggs
½ cup butter, softened
1 cup caster sugar
½ cup milk
2 cups self-raising flour, sifted
1 teaspoon vanilla extract
½ cup peanuts, crushed

Butter Cream Topping
1½ cups icing sugar
½ cup butter, room temperature

Meringue Topping
3 egg whites
¼ teaspoon cream of tartar
½ cup sugar

Toffee
½ caster sugar

1 Preheat the oven to 160°C. Line a 12-cupcake pan, with cupcake papers. In a medium-sized bowl, lightly beat the eggs, add butter and sugar, then mix until light and fluffy.

2 Add milk, flour and vanilla, and stir to combine. Beat with an electric mixer for 2 minutes, until light and creamy. Fold in crushed peanuts.

3 Divide the mixture evenly between the cake papers. Bake for 18–20 minutes until risen and firm to touch. Allow to cool for a few minutes and then transfer to a wire rack. Allow to cool fully before icing.

Butter Cream Topping

1 Meanwhile, combine half the icing sugar and butter, mix with a wooden spoon, add remaining sugar and butter and beat with the spoon until light and fluffy. Spread onto cupcakes.

Meringue Topping

1 Create a double boiler by bringing 2 cups of water to the boil in a medium-sized saucepan, and reduce heat slightly. Place a glass bowl into the saucepan that is large enough to fit into the pan while still resting on the top rim.

2 Add the egg whites to the hot bowl and whisk until foaming. Add cream of tartar and whisk until fluffy. Pour in the sugar slowly in one stream, whisking constantly to form stiff peaks.

3 Spread mixture onto a baking sheet and lightly brown under the grill for 1–2 minutes. Place in the oven for 3 minutes, then open the oven door slightly and leave meringue for a further 3 minutes.

Toffee

1 Place ½ cup caster sugar evenly on a greaseproof paper-lined baking tray, and bake in oven on 200°C for approximately 25 minutes until toffee consistency forms. Cool until hardened.

Makes 12

Playtime Cupcakes

Preparation 12 mins **Cooking** 20 mins **Calories** 354 **Fat** 18g **Carbohydrate** 45g

3 eggs
½ cup butter, softened
1 cup caster sugar
½ cup milk
1½ cups self-raising flour, sifted
1 teaspoon vanilla extract

Topping
200g coloured fondant
gel icing

1 Preheat the oven to 160°C. Line a 12-cupcake pan with cupcake papers. In a medium-sized bowl, lightly beat the eggs, add butter and sugar, then mix until light and fluffy.
2 Add milk, flour and vanilla, and stir to combine. Beat with an electric mixer for 2 minutes, until light and creamy.
3 Divide the mixture evenly between the cake papers. Bake for 18–20 minutes until risen and firm to touch. Allow to cool for a few minutes and then transfer to a wire rack. Allow to cool fully before icing.

Topping
1 Meanwhile, using a rolling pin roll out the fondant to 3mm thick. Using a biscuit cutter or sharp small knife, cut small circles and use to top cupcakes. Draw numbers on top with the gel icing.

Makes 12

Choc Chic Cupcakes

Preparation 12 mins **Cooking** 20 mins **Calories** 461 **Fat** 29g **Carbohydrate** 46g

3 eggs
½ cup butter, softened
1 cup caster sugar
½ cup milk
1½ cups self-raising flour, sifted
1 teaspoon vanilla extract
200g dark chocolate pieces
1 tablespoon cocoa powder

Topping
200g dark chocolate
⅓ cup cream, thickened
novelty chickens (available from cake decoration shops)

1 Preheat the oven to 160°C. Line a 12-cupcake pan with cupcake papers. In a medium-sized bowl, lightly beat the eggs, add butter and sugar, then mix until light and fluffy.

2 Add milk, flour and vanilla, and stir to combine. Add remaining ingredients. Beat with an electric mixer for 2 minutes, until light and creamy.

3 Divide the mixture evenly between the cake papers. Bake for 18–20 minutes until risen and firm to touch. Allow to cool for a few minutes and then transfer to a wire rack. Allow to cool fully before icing.

Topping

1 Meanwhile, combine the chocolate and cream in a medium-sized saucepan over a medium heat. As the mixture begins to melt, reduce heat to low, stirring constantly, until mixture melts and thickens. Remove from heat and cool.

2 Spoon chocolate mixture onto cupcake. Add novelty chickens to the top of each cupcake.

Makes 12

Chrissy Cups

Preparation 12 mins **Cooking** 20 mins **Calories** 386 **Fat** 46g **Carbohydrate** 21g

3 eggs
½ cup unsalted butter
½ cup sugar
⅓ cup unsweetened pineapple juice
1 cup plain flour, sifted
1½ cups candied fruits,
finely chopped
⅔ cup raisins, chopped
¼ cup pitted dates, finely chopped
¾ teaspoon baking powder
½ teaspoon salt
½ teaspoon vanilla extract

Topping
1½ cups icing sugar
1 teaspoon lemon essence
½ cup butter, room temperature
1 tablespoon brandy
candied novelty holly
(available from specialist
cake decoration stores)

1 Preheat the oven to 160°C. Line a 12-cupcake pan with cupcake papers. In a medium-sized bowl, lightly beat the eggs, add butter and sugar, then mix until light and fluffy.

2 Add pineapple juice and flour, and stir to combine. Add remaining ingredients. Beat with an electric mixer for 2 minutes, until light and creamy.

3 Divide the mixture evenly between the cake papers. Bake for 18–20 minutes until risen and firm to touch. Allow to cool for a few minutes and then transfer to a wire rack. Allow to cool fully before icing.

Topping

1 Meanwhile, combine half quantities of all the topping ingredients except for the novelty holly, and mix with a wooden spoon. Add remaining ingredients and beat with the spoon until light and fluffy.

2 Put icing into a piping bag with a medium-sized plain nozzle and pipe onto fruit cakes. Top with candied novelty holly.

Makes 12

Chai Chai Cupcakes

Preparation 12 mins **Cooking** 25 mins **Calories** 326 **Fat** 18g **Carbohydrate** 39g

¼ cup chai mixture (Indian spiced tea)

¼ cup hot water

3 eggs

½ cup butter, softened

1 cup caster sugar

¼ cup milk

1½ cups self-raising flour, sifted

1 teaspoon vanilla extract

1 teaspoon cinnamon

1 teaspoon nutmeg

Topping

¼ cup raw sugar

2 tablespoons warm water

cinnamon sugar

12 star anises

1   Preheat the oven to 160°C. Line a 12 cupcake pan with cup cake papers.

2   In a small bowl, add hot water to the spiced tea mixture, stand for 15 minutes, strain and set aside. In a medium-sized bowl, lightly beat the eggs, add butter and sugar, then mix until light and fluffy.

3   Add milk and flour, and stir to combine. Add remaining ingredients. Beat with an electric mixer for 2 minutes, until light and creamy. Add chai tea to mix and stir through.

4   Divide the mixture evenly between the cake papers. Bake for 18–20 minutes until risen and firm to touch. Allow to cool for a few minutes and then transfer to a wire rack. Allow to cool fully before icing.

Topping

1   Meanwhile, combine the raw sugar and water in a small bowl, mix with a wooden spoon, spoon onto cupcakes and sprinkle with cinnamon sugar. Decorate each cupcake with a single star anise.

Makes 12

Sticky Date Cupcakes

Preparation 12 mins **Cooking** 20 mins **Calories** 322 **Fat** 13g **Carbohydrate** 50g

2 eggs

¾ cup butter, room temperature

¾ cup caster sugar

1 cup self-raising flour, sifted

¾ cup water

400g dates, chopped

2 teaspoons instant coffee powder

1 teaspoon bicarbonate of soda

1 teaspoon vanilla extract

1 cup ground almond flour

½ cup walnuts, finely chopped

Topping

1 cup packed light-brown sugar

⅓ cup unsalted butter

20mL water

1 teaspoon vanilla extract

50g dates

1. Preheat the oven to 160°C. Line a 12-cupcake pan with cupcake papers. In a medium-sized bowl, lightly beat the eggs, add butter and sugar, then mix until light and fluffy.
2. Add water and flour, and stir to combine. Add remaining ingredients. Mix with a wooden spoon for 2 minutes, until light and creamy.
3. Divide the mixture evenly between the cake papers. Bake for 18–20 minutes until risen and firm to touch. Allow to cool for a few minutes and then transfer to a wire rack. Allow to cool fully before icing.

Topping

1. Meanwhile, combine sugar, butter, water and vanilla in a saucepan. Bring to a simmer over medium-low heat, stirring constantly. Without stirring again, simmer for 1 minute. Remove from heat, allow to cool and spoon onto cakes. Top each cupcake with a date and more sugar mixture. Heat the top of each cupcake with a blowtorch, being careful not to scorch the paper or the dates.

Makes 12

Pecan Coffee Crunch Cupcakes

Preparation 12 mins **Cooking** 20 mins **Calories** 505 **Fat** 33g **Carbohydrate** 50g

3 eggs
½ cup butter, softened
1 cup caster sugar
¼ cup milk
1½ cups self-raising flour, sifted
1 tablespoon espresso or instant coffee
½ cup pecans, chopped
1 tablespoon golden syrup

Topping
1 cup packed light-brown sugar
⅓ cup unsalted butter
20mL water
1 teaspoon vanilla extract
100g pecans

1 Preheat the oven to 160°C. Line a 12-cupcake pan with cupcake papers. In a medium-sized bowl, lightly beat the eggs, add butter and sugar, then mix until light and fluffy.

2 Add milk and flour, and stir to combine. Add remaining ingredients. Mix with a wooden spoon for 2 minutes, until light and creamy.

3 Divide the mixture evenly between the cake papers. Bake for 18–20 minutes until risen and firm to touch. Allow to cool for a few minutes and then transfer to a wire rack. Allow to cool fully before icing.

Topping

1 Meanwhile, combine sugar, butter, water and vanilla in a saucepan. Bring to a simmer over medium-low heat, stirring constantly. Without stirring again, simmer 1 minute. Remove from heat, add pecans, allow to cool slightly and spoon onto cakes in mounds.

Makes 12

Caramel Nougat Cupcakes

Preparation 12 mins **Cooking** 20 mins **Calories** 325 **Fat** 19g **Carbohydrate** 38g

3 eggs
½ cup butter, softened
1 cup caster sugar
½ cup milk
1½ cups self-raising flour
1 teaspoon vanilla extract

Topping
1½ cups icing sugar
½ cup butter, room temperature
100g nougat

1 Preheat the oven to 160°C. Line a 12-cupcake pan with cupcake papers. In a medium-sized bowl, lightly beat the eggs, add butter and sugar, then mix until light and fluffy.

2 Add milk, flour and vanilla, and stir to combine. Beat with an electric mixer for 2 minutes, until light and creamy.

3 Divide the mixture evenly between the cake papers. Bake for 18–20 minutes until risen and firm to touch. Allow to cool for a few minutes and then transfer to a wire rack. Allow to cool fully before icing.

Topping

1 Meanwhile, combine icing sugar and butter in a small bowl, mix, and add chopped nougat. Stir and spoon onto cupcakes in mounds.

Makes 12

Pistachio Zinger Cupcakes

Preparation 12 mins **Cooking** 20 mins **Calories** 478 **Fat** 32g **Carbohydrate** 45g

3 eggs
½ cup butter, softened
1 cup caster sugar
½ cup yoghurt
2 cups self-raising flour, sifted
1 teaspoon vanilla extract
1 zucchini, grated
juice of ½ a lime
zest of 1 lime
½ cup pistachio nuts

Topping
1½ cups icing sugar
½ cup butter, room temperature
zest of 1 lime
½ cup pistachio nuts

1 Preheat the oven to 160°C. Line a 12-cupcake pan with cupcake papers. In a medium-sized bowl, lightly beat the eggs, add butter and sugar, then mix until light and fluffy.

2 Add yoghurt, flour and vanilla, and stir to combine. Beat with an electric mixer for 2 minutes, until light and creamy. Add zucchini, lime juice, zest and pistachio nuts and mix through.

3 Divide the mixture evenly between the cake papers. Bake for 18–20 minutes until risen and firm to touch. Allow to cool for a few minutes and then transfer to a wire rack. Allow to cool fully before icing.

Topping

1 Meanwhile, combine half the icing sugar and butter, mix with a wooden spoon, then add remaining icing sugar and butter, and beat with the spoon until light and fluffy. Add lime zest and half of the pistachios and mix through.

2 Apply icing to cupcakes with the back of a spoon or a small spatula, and sprinkle each cake with a few of the remaining nuts.

Makes 12

Hazelnut Express Cupcakes

Preparation 12 mins **Cooking** 20 mins **Calories** 500 **Fat** 38g **Carbohydrate** 44g

3 eggs
½ cup butter, softened
1 cup caster sugar
½ cup milk
1 cup self-raising flour, sifted
¼ teaspoon baking powder
½ cup hazelnut meal
½ cup hazelnuts, chopped
¼ cup cocoa powder
2 tablespoons instant coffee powder

Topping
1½ cups icing sugar
½ cup unsalted butter
1 tablespoon hazelnut liqueur
12 coffee beans

1 Preheat the oven to 160°C. Line a 12-cupcake pan with cupcake papers. In a medium-sized bowl, lightly beat the eggs, add butter and sugar, then mix until light and fluffy.

2 Add milk and flour, and stir to combine. Add remaining cake ingredients. Mix with a wooden spoon for 2 minutes, until light and creamy.

3 Divide the mixture evenly between the cake papers. Bake for 18–20 minutes until risen and firm to touch. Allow to cool for a few minutes and then transfer to a wire rack. Allow to cool fully before icing.

Topping

1 Meanwhile, combine all topping ingredients except for coffee beans in a small bowl, mix with wooden spoon, and spoon onto cupcakes. Decorate each cake with a coffee bean.

Makes 12

Marmalade Pecan Cupcakes

Preparation 12 mins   **Cooking** 20 mins   **Calories** 356   **Fat** 21g   **Carbohydrate** 40g

3 eggs
½ cup butter, softened
1 cup caster sugar
¼ cup milk
1½ cups self-raising flour, sifted
½ teaspoon cocoa powder
zest of 1 small orange
juice of 1 small orange
¼ cup pecans, chopped

Topping
1½ cups icing sugar
½ cup butter, room temperature
¼ cup orange juice
2 tablespoons marmalade
12 pecan pieces

1 Preheat the oven to 160°C. Line a 12-cupcake pan with cupcake papers. In a medium-sized bowl, lightly beat the eggs, add butter and sugar, then mix until light and fluffy.

2 Add milk, flour and cocoa powder, and stir to combine. Beat with an electric mixer for 2 minutes, until light and creamy. Add zest, juice and nuts, and stir.

3 Divide the mixture evenly between the cake papers. Bake for 18–20 minutes until risen and firm to touch. Allow to cool for a few minutes and then transfer to a wire rack. Allow to cool fully before icing.

Topping

1 Meanwhile, combine icing sugar, butter and orange juice into a bowl; beat with a whisk until light and fluffy. Combine with marmalade. Spoon glaze over the cupcakes and top with a pecan piece.

Makes 12

Introduction

Cheesecakes are among the most popular traditional treats available – from Continental delights to intriguing Middle Eastern flavours, you will find cheesy desserts from all over the globe.

We have assembled Old World recipes, New World recipes and an exotic mix of tropical and Eastern recipes for you to try. This is not a slimming cookbook, that's for sure, but remember that everything in moderation leads to a happy as well as a healthy existence. So while you should not be reaching for this cookbook on a daily basis, there is nothing wrong with the occasional tasty indulgence, particularly when they are as tasty and indulgent as the recipes on offer here!

We have included elegant single-serve recipes among the larger classic cheesecakes – this makes it easier to divide or multiply these recipes to make as many or as few as you like. Individual cheesecakes make for a great visual display if you are having a dinner party, and they also pack and travel well for picnics and lunches.

For the more traditional at heart, you will find wonderful well-known American and Continental treats along with exotic and perfumed offerings from further afield.

Among the Eastern recipes you will encounter cheeses you may not be familiar with – if you do not live in an area where Turkish, Lebanese or Middle Eastern foods are readily available, they can be substituted with ricotta. However, it is well worth asking around as you may be surprised by what is available beyond your regular supermarket, and you will definitely enjoy and benefit from such a culinary excursion. For the tropical cheesecake section try your local Chinatown or Asian grocery stores and be guided by what looks good and is in season.

Remember – fresh is always best.

The Basics

To get started, there are a few basic dos and don'ts when it comes to baking most desserts. Fortunately in the case of set cheesecakes, if you follow the recipe provided you should have a fail-safe delicious treat on your hands in as much time as it takes your cheesecake to set in the refrigerator.

Equipment

A small selection of mixing bowls, wooden spoons and whisks should suffice for the preparation of basic cheesecake fillings and toppings, although if you have an electric mixer and a few spatulas, you will definitely find them useful. If you already have some cake tins and tart moulds, use what you have – just make sure the base is a separate removable piece from the sides or that the side will open to release your cheesecake when it is ready.

If you are in the market for new cake tins, choose good-quality springform tins and purchase a few different sizes. A handful of small single-serve springform tins is also a great investment. Non-stick tins will give you years of effortless use if you treat them well, and remember to never cut or scrape them with metal knives or spatulas. Wash them by hand and keep metal scourers away from them as well. Looking after and preparing your tins correctly is the first step on the way to a good end result.

When using springform tins, whether a recipe calls for buttering or oiling a cake tin or not, do so regardless, making thoroughly sure that the entire surface has been buttered. A light dusting of plain flour over the buttered surface guarantees an easy release after baking. If a recipe calls for coating the buttered surface with ground nuts, biscuit crumbs or coconut, omit the light dusting of flour.

There is a sure-fire way of getting a cake out of a springform tin quickly and easily: before filling the tin, simply remove the sides and place a large piece of baking paper over the base. Replace the sides and close the hinge, creating a tight false bottom on the base of the tin. Once the cake has baked and the sides of the tin can be removed, place the cake on a platter and slide the cake tin base out. Next, cut away the overhanging paper from one side, cutting as close as possible to the cheesecake. Gently pull the paper from the opposite side – it is a good idea to gently rest a large knife or spatula along the side that you are pulling the paper from so you do not tear the cheesecake at all.

Quality scales and measuring cups are a major help. Make sure you choose measuring cups where the metric cup measures 250mL. Small, nested sets of measuring cups are also useful, as are tablespoon and teaspoon measures. If investing in baking equipment, for absolute ease of measuring purchase scales that can measure liquid as well as dry ingredients.

It is also a good idea to make sure that your oven heats accurately. To check, purchase an oven thermometer and heat your oven to 200°C. Place the oven thermometer inside and leave it for 30 minutes. Remove the thermometer and check that it registers within 5°C. If not, it may be time to call a serviceman to re-adjust the oven temperature.

Ingredients

Quality ingredients are always important. Make sure your flour is fresh, especially if using wholemeal or rye flour. To check, stir a spoonful or two into a glass of warm water. The aroma should be pleasantly floury, not bitter or sour.

Purchase good-quality cocoa and chocolate, and store nuts in an airtight container away from the light, or in the freezer so they remain at their best for as long as possible. Buy coconut as necessary and make sure that cream, buttermilk and all other dairy products are fresh. When using fresh fruit in recipes, ensure they are firm or soft, as the recipe dictates. For example, using a firm banana where a soft one is called for will change the essence of the recipe. And where possible, always buy what's in season and not just what is in the supermarket – this way you will get well-priced, quality ingredients every time.

American Cheesecakes

The United States has developed its own distinct repertoire of cheesecakes, typified by the classic New York-style, but many others often feature chocolate, berries or even Bourbon. For those of us with a real sweet tooth, look no further than a toffee, chocolate caramel, or rocky road cheesecake.

Chocolate Caramel Cheesecake

Base

150g digestive biscuits, finely crushed

50g butter, melted

Filling

¼ cup evaporated milk

380g canned caramel

1 cup pecans, chopped

500g cream cheese

½ cup sugar

2 eggs

1 teaspoon vanilla extract

¾ cup chocolate chips, melted

1 Preheat oven to 180°C.

Base

2 Combine crumbs and melted butter. Press mixture evenly into a 23cm springform tin. Bake for 8 minutes. Remove from oven and allow to cool.

Filling

3 Combine milk and caramel in a heavy-based saucepan. Cook over low heat until melted, stirring often. Pour over biscuit base. Sprinkle pecans evenly over caramel layer and set aside.

4 Beat cream cheese at high speed with electric mixer until light and fluffy. Gradually add sugar, mixing well. Add eggs one at a time, beating well after each addition. Stir in vanilla and melted chocolate, beat until blended. Pour over pecan layer.

5 Bake for 30 minutes. Remove from oven and run knife around edge of tin to release sides. Cool to room temperature. Cover and chill for 8 hours.

6 Decorate with a chopped flaky chocolate bar and chopped jersey caramels. Serve with whipped cream.

12 Slices

American Jaffa Cheesecake

Base

60g digestive biscuits, finely crushed

30g butter, melted

¼ cup sugar

Filling

500g cream cheese, softened

2 tablespoons orange juice

finely grated zest of 1 large orange

¼ cup sugar

2 large eggs

½ cup chocolate chips

1 Preheat oven to 165°C.

Base

2 Combine crumbs, butter and sugar. Line four 10cm springform tins with baking paper, then press mixture evenly onto bottoms of tins.

3 Bake for 5 minutes.

Filling

4 Combine cream cheese, juice, zest and sugar in an electric mixer, mix on medium speed until well combined. Add eggs one at a time. Stir through the chocolate. Divide filling evenly between tins.

5 Bake for 25 minutes. Cool before removing from tins.

Serves 4

Frozen Peppermint Cheesecake

Base

300g mint slice biscuits

Filling

250g cream cheese, softened

400g condensed milk

1 cup hard peppermint sweets, crushed

2 cups thickened cream, whipped

Base

1 Place mint slices into a food processor and process until fine. Firmly press onto bottom of a 23cm springform tin. Chill.

Filling

2 Beat cream cheese at high speed with an electric mixer until fluffy. Add condensed milk and peppermint sweets. Beat well, then fold in whipped cream. Pour over base. Cover and freeze until firm.

3 Decorate with peppermint crisp bar and serve.

12 Slices

Key Lime Cheesecake

Base

150g digestive biscuits, finely crushed

2 tablespoons sugar

50g butter, melted

Filling

570g cream cheese, softened

¾ cup sugar

1 cup sour cream

3 tablespoons plain flour

3 large eggs

¾ cup fresh lime juice

1 teaspoon vanilla extract

Candied Lime

1½ cups caster sugar

3–4 fresh limes, thinly sliced

1 Preheat oven to 190°C.

Base

2 In a bowl, combine the crumbs and sugar, then stir in the butter well. Pat the mixture evenly onto the bottom and 1cm up the sides of a buttered 25cm springform tin. Bake the base in the centre of the oven for 8 minutes. Transfer the pan to a rack and set aside to cool.

Filling

3 Beat together the cream cheese and sugar with an electric mixer until smooth. Beat in the sour cream and flour, then add the eggs one at a time, beating well after each addition.

4 Add the lime juice and vanilla, and beat until smooth. Pour the filling over the base. Bake for 15 minutes, reduce the temperature to 120°C and bake for 50–55 minutes more, or until the centre is barely set. Allow to cool on a rack, then refrigerate, covered, overnight.

5 Remove the cheesecake from the tin and transfer it to a plate.

Candied lime

6 Place 1 cup water and 1 cup of the sugar in a pan. Boil until the sugar dissolves. Add the lime slices and simmer for 10 minutes. Meanwhile place the rest of the sugar on a tray.

7 Remove the limes from the heat, strain and dry on absorbent paper. Cool slightly, then place one at a time on the tray of sugar to coat. Place around the edge of the cheesecake and serve.

12 Slices

Cheesecake Cookies

Base

70g butter, softened
⅓ cup brown sugar, packed
1 cup plain flour

Filling

½ cup sugar
250g cream cheese, softened
1 egg
2 tablespoons milk
1 tablespoon lemon juice
½ teaspoon vanilla extract

1 Preheat oven to 180°C.

Base

2 In a medium bowl, blend the butter, brown sugar and flour with a fork until mixture resembles coarse crumbs.

3 Put 1 cup of the mixture aside for topping. Press remaining mixture into a 20 x 20 x 5cm baking dish, bake for 15 minutes. Remove from oven and allow to cool.

Filling

4 In another bowl combine sugar and cream cheese, mixing until smooth. Thoroughly beat in egg, milk, lemon juice and vanilla. Spread over the baked base and sprinkle with remaining brown sugar mixture. Bake for 25 minutes. Cool, then chill for at least 1 hour. Cut into 12 squares.

Serves 12

New York-Style Cheesecake

Base

120g digestive biscuits, finely crushed

¾ cup sugar

50g butter, melted

Filling

1½ cups sour cream

1 cup sugar

2 eggs

1 teaspoon vanilla extract

500g cream cheese, broken into small pieces

40g butter, melted

1 Preheat oven to 165°C.

Base

2 Blend the biscuit crumbs, sugar and melted butter, then line the bottom of an ungreased 23cm springform tin.

Filling

3 Blend the sour cream, sugar, eggs and vanilla in a food processor for 1 minute. Add the cream cheese, blend until smooth. While blending, pour the melted butter through the top of the machine. Pour cream cheese mixture into the springform tin.

4 Bake in the lower third of the oven for 45 minutes, remove from oven and cool.

5 Refrigerate for at least 4 hours, preferably overnight. Dust with plenty of icing sugar before cutting and serving. Serve with whipped cream.

12 Slices

Sultana and Bourbon Cheesecake

Base
60g digestive biscuits, finely crushed
30g butter, melted
¼ cup sugar

Filling
1½ cups raisins
¼ cup Bourbon
500g cream cheese, softened
¼ cup sugar
1 tablespoon lemon juice
zest of ½ lemon
2 large eggs

1 Soak the raisins in the Bourbon for at least 2 hours. Preheat oven to 165°C.

Base

2 Combine crumbs, butter and sugar. Line four 10cm springform tins with baking paper, then press mixture evenly onto bottoms of tins. Bake for 5 minutes.

Filling

3 Combine cream cheese, sugar, juice and zest in an electric mixer, mix on medium speed until well blended. Add eggs one at a time, mixing thoroughly between additions. Chop 1 cup of the soaked raisins roughly and add to the filling, then divide filling evenly between tins.

4 Bake for 25 minutes. Cool before removing from tins, then chill.

5 Let stand at room temperature for minimum of 40 minutes. Decorate with the remaining raisins and serve with whipped cream.

Serves 4

Linseed Cheesecake with Berries

Base

1 cup ground linseed

60g digestive biscuits, finely crushed

45g butter, melted

Filling

250g cottage cheese

2 cups plain yoghurt

½ cup raw sugar

1 tablespoon plain flour

1 whole egg

2 egg whites

2 teaspoons vanilla extract

125g fresh blueberries

125g fresh raspberries

1 Preheat oven to 180°C.

Base

2 Mix linseed, biscuits and butter together until combined. Press into an 20cm springform tin.

3 Bake for 10 minutes. Cool on a rack. Reduce oven temperature to 150°C.

Filling

4 In a blender or food processor, blend the cottage cheese and yoghurt for at least 1 minute. Add sugar, flour, whole egg, egg whites and vanilla. Blend until smooth.

5 Pour filling into base. Bake until top feels dry when lightly touched, approximately 60 minutes. Cool completely.

6 Decorate cheesecake with fresh blueberries and raspberries. Serve with extra berries on the side.

12 Slices

Rocky Road Cheesecake

Base
¾ cup ground almonds

20g butter, melted

Filling
1½ tablespoons gelatine

450g cream cheese

¾ cup milk

¾ cup sugar

¼ teaspoon vanilla extract

200g rocky road, chopped into small pieces

Base

1 Stir together almonds and butter in a small bowl.

2 Line four 10cm springform tins with baking paper, then press mixture evenly onto bottoms of tins.

Filling

3 Soften gelatine in ¼ cup water in a small saucepan, stir over low heat until dissolved. Beat cream cheese, milk, sugar and vanilla with an electric mixer until well blended. Stir in half the rocky road then the gelatine. Divide filling evenly between tins, place in refrigerator for 3 hours or overnight.

4 Decorate with extra rocky road and serve.

Serves 4

Pecan Cheesecake

Base

180g digestive biscuits,
finely crushed

3 tablespoons sugar

50g butter, melted

Filling

1¼kg cream cheese, softened

1⅔ cups light brown sugar,
firmly packed

40g butter, melted

5 eggs

1 teaspoon vanilla extract

1 cup pecans, chopped

1 Preheat oven to 165°C.

Base

2 Combine biscuits, sugar and butter, mixing well. Press into bottom of 25cm springform tin, chill.

Filling

3 Beat cream cheese in an electric mixer until light and fluffy, gradually add brown sugar and butter, mixing well. Add eggs, one at a time, beating well after each addition. Stir in vanilla and pecans. Spoon filling into tin and bake for 1 hour.

4 Turn oven off. Allow cheesecake to cool in oven for 30 minutes. Cool to room temperature then refrigerate for 8 hours. Remove sides of springform tin.

5 Decorate with extra pecans and serve with whipped cream.

12 Slices

White Chocolate Cheesecake with Raspberry Sauce

Filling
1 cup white chocolate chips
500g cream cheese, softened
¾ cup sugar
3 eggs
1½ teaspoons vanilla extract
¾ cup sour cream

Raspberry Sauce
½ cup sugar
2½ cups raspberries
½ cup thickened cream, whipped

1 Preheat oven to 165°C.

Filling

2 Place chocolate in a double boiler and heat over hot water until it melts. Stir to blend, then cool to room temperature.

3 With an electric mixer, blend cream cheese and sugar until smooth. Mix in eggs, vanilla and sour cream. Stir in melted chocolate – it is important to have the cheesecake ingredients and the melted chocolate close to the same temperature when they are combined so that they blend together smoothly.

4 Pour into a greased 23cm springform tin. Bake in the middle of the oven for 25 minutes or until just barely set. Turn off the oven, leave the door ajar, and allow to cool in oven for 1 hour longer. Chill.

Raspberry Sauce

5 Place sugar and ½ cup water in a saucepan, bring to the boil and simmer for 5 minutes. Meanwhile, purée 2 cups of the raspberries in a blender. Add the puréed raspberries to the sugar syrup, simmer for another 3 minutes. Remove from heat and cool.

6 Pipe cream onto the cheesecake and top with the remaining raspberries. Serve with the raspberry sauce.

12 Slices

Blueberry Cheesecake

Base

100g macadamias, finely chopped
in blender
1 cup plain flour
¼ cup brown sugar, firmly packed
90g butter, softened

Filling

750g cream cheese, softened
1½ teaspoons vanilla extract
1¼ cups sugar
4 eggs at room temperature
1 cup sour cream

Topping

¾ cup sugar
½ tablespoon gelatine
250g fresh blueberries

1 Preheat oven to 200°C.

Base

2 Combine base ingredients and mix well, press onto bottom of 25cm springform tin.

3 Bake for 10–15 minutes. Remove from oven and allow to cool. Reduce oven temperature to 180°C.

Filling

4 Crumble cream cheese into an electric mixer. Add 1 teaspoon of the vanilla and 1 cup of the sugar, then add eggs one at a time, mixing well on high speed after each addition. Mix until blended and smooth, about 4 minutes. Pour over base.

5 Bake for 30 minutes until set but not completely firm. Remove from oven, cool for 10 minutes.

6 Combine sour cream with remaining sugar and vanilla. Spread over cheesecake. Bake for 5 minutes.

Topping

7 In a saucepan, place ½ cup water and the sugar, bring to a boil and reduce for 10 minutes. Meanwhile, dissolve the gelatine in ¼ cup warm water. Add the blueberries to the sugar syrup, stir, then add the gelatine mixture. Stir and pour over the cooled cheesecake.

12 Slices

Baked Cherry Cheesecake

Base

60g digestive biscuits, finely crushed

1 tablespoon sugar

¼ teaspoon ground cinnamon

¼ teaspoon nutmeg

Filling

5 eggs

1 cup sugar

500g cream cheese, softened

1 cup sour cream

2 tablespoons plain flour

1 teaspoon vanilla extract

Glaze

425g canned black cherries

150g black cherry jam

½ cup sugar

1 Preheat oven to 135°C.

Base

2 Butter a 23cm springform tin and line with baking paper.

3 Combine biscuit crumbs, sugar, cinnamon and nutmeg and sprinkle evenly over tin. Set aside.

Filling

4 Separate eggs and beat yolks until lemon coloured, then gradually add sugar. Cut cream cheese into tiny chunks, beat until smooth, then slowly add egg yolk mixture. Beat until smooth, then add sour cream, flour and vanilla. Beat again until smooth. Beat egg whites until stiff but not dry. Gently fold egg whites into cream cheese mixture. Pour into prepared tin and bake for 70 minutes.

5 Turn off heat and leave in oven for 1 hour longer without opening oven door.

Glaze

6 Drain the cherries and place ½ cup of the liquid with the jam and sugar in a saucepan, bring to the boil and reduce by half. Add the cherries and simmer for a further 3 minutes. Cool and pour over the cooled cheesecake.

12 Slices

Toffee Cheesecake

Base

100g vanilla wafers, finely crushed
90g butter, melted

Filling

400g caramel sweets
1 cup semi-sweet chocolate chips
½ cup evaporated milk
3 chocolate bars covered in toffee, 40g each
1kg cream cheese
1½ cups sugar
2 tablespoons plain flour, plus 2 teaspoons
4 whole eggs
2 egg yolks
⅓ cup double cream

1 Preheat oven to 175°C.

Base

2 In a medium-size bowl combine wafer crumbs with the melted butter. Mix well. Press onto bottom and sides of a 23cm springform tin. Bake for 10 minutes, remove and allow to cool.

Filling

3 Increase oven temperature to 200°C. In a saucepan over low heat, melt caramels together with the chocolate chips and evaporated milk, stir until smooth and pour into base. Break the chocolate bars into small pieces and sprinkle over the caramel layer.

4 Beat cream cheese until smooth. Add sugar and flour and beat until smooth. Add whole eggs and egg yolks one at a time, mixing well after each addition. Blend in cream, then pour over caramel and toffee layers. Wrap outside of pan with foil.

5 Set in a large pan that has been filled with 1¼cm of hot water. Bake for 15 minutes, reduce oven to 110°C and bake for another hour. Remove from water, cool to room temperature then chill overnight in the refrigerator.

6 Top with whipped cream and chocolate caramel sweets to serve.

12 Slices

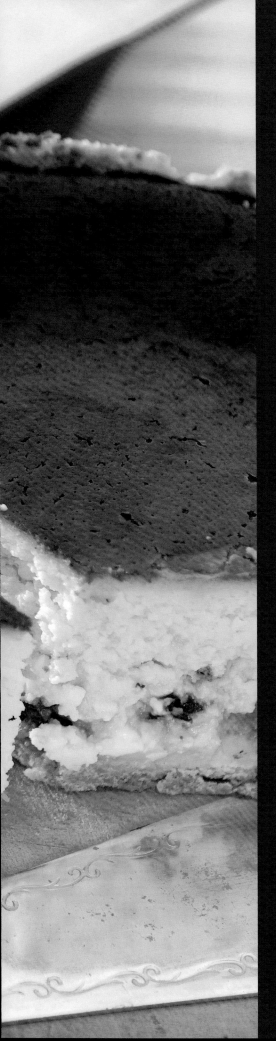

Continental
Cheesecakes

In this chapter you will find not only time-honoured recipes from Europe's long tradition of cheesecakes, but also newer innovations, both of which often make use of berry, almond or vanilla flavours. Traditional cheesecakes such as German and Italian can be found next to latecomers like hazelnut raspberry and the playful cheesecake brûlée.

Raspberry Cheesecake

Base

60g digestive biscuits, finely crushed

30g butter, melted

¼ cup sugar

Filling

500g cream cheese, softened

1 tablespoon lemon juice

1 teaspoon vanilla extract

¼ cup sugar

2 large eggs

125g fresh raspberries

1 Preheat oven to 165°C.

Base

2 Combine crumbs, butter and sugar. Line four 10cm springform tins with baking paper, then press mixture evenly onto bottoms of tins.

3 Bake for 5 minutes.

Filling

4 Combine cream cheese, juice, vanilla and sugar in an electric mixer, mix on medium speed until well combined. Add the eggs one at a time, mixing well after each addition. Gently fold through ¾ of the raspberries. Divide filling evenly between each base. Top cheesecakes with the remaining raspberries.

5 Bake for 25 minutes. Cool before removing from tins.

Serves 4

Hazelnut Raspberry Cheesecake

Base

190g amaretti biscuits, finely crushed

60g butter, melted

Filling

1kg cream cheese, softened

1¼ cups sugar

3 large eggs

1 cup sour cream

1 teaspoon vanilla extract

170g hazelnut spread

⅓ cup raspberry conserve

1 Preheat oven to 165°C.

Base

2 Combine crumbs and butter, press onto bottom of 23cm springform tin.

Filling

3 Combine ¾ of the cream cheese and the sugar in an electric mixer and mix on medium speed until well blended. Add eggs one at a time, beating well after each addition. Blend in sour cream and vanilla, pour over base.

4 Combine remaining cream cheese and the hazelnut spread in the electric mixer, mix on medium speed until well blended. Add raspberry conserve, mix well.

5 Drop heaped tablespoonfuls of hazelnut mixture into plain cream cheese filling – do not swirl.

6 Bake for 1 hour and 25 minutes. Loosen cake from rim of tin, cool before removing. Serve with fresh raspberries.

12 Slices

Continental Nougat Cheesecake

Base

¾ cup ground almonds

20g butter, melted

Filling

1½ tablespoons gelatine

450g cream cheese

¾ cup milk

¾ cup sugar

2 teaspoons almond extract

100g nougat, cut into small pieces

Base

1 Stir together almonds and butter in a small bowl.

2 Line four 10cm springform tins with baking paper, then press mixture evenly onto bottoms of tins.

Filling

3 Soften gelatine in ¼ cup water in a small saucepan, stir over low heat until dissolved. Beat cream cheese, milk, sugar and almond extract with an electric mixer until well blended. Stir in the gelatine. Divide filling evenly between tins, place in refrigerator for 3 hours or overnight.

4 Top each cheesecake with nougat pieces and serve.

Serves 4

Ricotta Cheesecake

Base

180g digestive biscuits, finely crushed

Filling

1⅓kg ricotta cheese, drained

2 cups sugar

8 egg yolks

½ cup plain flour, sifted

zest of 1 lemon

1 teaspoon vanilla extract

8 egg whites

½ cup thickened cream, whipped

1 Preheat oven to 220°C.

Base

2 Sprinkle a 30cm springform tin with the biscuit crumbs.

Filling

3 Beat ricotta until smooth, gradually add ¾ of the sugar, then add egg yolks one at a time, mixing well after each addition. Beat in flour, lemon zest and vanilla.

4 Beat egg whites with remaining sugar. Fold whipped cream and egg whites into ricotta mixture and turn into prepared tin. Bake for 10 minutes, lower temperature to 180°C and bake for 1 hour. Turn off heat and allow to cool in oven with door closed. Dust with icing sugar before serving.

12 Slices

Cappuccino Cheesecake

Base
1½ cups finely chopped nuts (almonds, walnuts)
2 tablespoons sugar
50g butter, melted

Filling
1kg cream cheese, softened
1 cup sugar
3 tablespoons plain flour
4 large eggs
1 cup sour cream
1 tablespoon instant coffee granules
¼ teaspoon ground cinnamon

1 Preheat oven to 160°C.

Base
2 Combine nuts, sugar and butter, press onto bottom of 23cm springform tin. Bake for 10 minutes, remove from oven and allow to cool. Increase oven temperature to 230°C.

Filling
3 Combine cream cheese, sugar and flour in an electric mixer, mix on medium speed until well blended. Add eggs, one at a time, mixing well after each addition. Blend in sour cream.

4 Dissolve coffee granules and cinnamon in ¼ cup boiling water. Cool, then gradually add to cream cheese mixture, mixing until well blended. Pour over base.

5 Bake for 10 minutes. Reduce oven temperature to 120°C and continue baking for 1 hour.

6 Loosen cake from rim, allow to cool before removing. Chill. Serve topped with whipped cream and coffee beans.

12 Slices

Lemon Cheesecake

Base
50g vanilla wafers, finely crushed
40g butter, melted
3 tablespoons sugar

Filling
340g cream cheese
½ cup lemon juice
½ cup sugar
2 eggs, beaten

Topping
1 cup sour cream
zest of 2 lemons
4 tablespoons sugar

1 Preheat oven to 180°C.

Base

2 Mix vanilla wafer crumbs, melted butter and sugar together. Press mixture firmly on bottom and sides of buttered 20cm springform tin.

Filling

3 Blend cream cheese and lemon juice, add sugar and beat until smooth. Add eggs one at a time, mixing thoroughly after each addition. Pour into base, then bake for 20 minutes or until firm. Remove from oven and cool for 5 minutes only.

Topping

4 Mix sour cream, grated lemon zest and sugar, then spread over cheesecake. Bake 10 minutes longer. Cool, chill in refrigerator for at least 5 hours before serving. Serve with whipped cream.

12 Slices

Fruits of the Forest Cheesecake

Base

60g digestive biscuits, finely crushed

30g butter, melted

¼ cup sugar

Filling

500g cream cheese, softened

1 tablespoon lemon juice

1 teaspoon vanilla extract

¼ cup sugar

2 large eggs

Topping

140g frozen mixed berries

½ cup strawberry jam

¼ cup sugar

1 Preheat oven to 165°C.

Base

2 Combine crumbs, butter and sugar. Line four 10cm springform tins with baking paper, then press mixture evenly onto bottoms of tins.

3 Bake for 5 minutes.

Filling

4 Combine cream cheese, juice, vanilla and sugar in an electric mixer, mix on medium speed until well combined. Add the eggs one at a time, mixing well after each addition. Pour filling over the base.

5 Bake for 25 minutes. Cool before removing from tins.

Topping

6 Meanwhile, in a small saucepan over a low heat combine the berries, jam and sugar. Simmer gently for 10 minutes, stirring occasionally. Remove from the heat and cool.

7 Once both the cheesecakes and the berries are cool, spoon the berry topping over each cheesecake and serve immediately.

Serves 4

Amaretto Cheesecake

½ cup whole almonds
500g cream cheese
¾ cup sugar
3 eggs
1 teaspoon vanilla extract
2 tablespoons Amaretto
¾ cup sour cream

1 Preheat oven to 170°C.

2 Spread nuts in a baking pan and bake for 8 minutes or until lightly toasted. Cool and finely chop.

3 With an electric mixer, beat cheese and sugar until smooth. Mix in eggs, vanilla, Amaretto and sour cream, then stir in nuts.

4 Pour cream cheese mixture into a buttered 23cm springform tin. Bake in the middle of the oven for 25 minutes or until just barely set.

5 Turn off the oven, leave the door ajar, and allow to cool in the oven for 1 hour longer. Chill.

6 To serve, remove tin sides and cut into wedges. Decorate with toasted flaked almonds.

12 Slices

Mini Currant and Lemon Cheesecake

Base
60g digestive biscuits,
finely crushed
30g butter, melted
¼ cup sugar

Filling
500g cream cheese, softened
2 tablespoons lemon juice
zest of 2 lemons
¼ cup sugar
2 large eggs
½ cup currants

Topping
finely grated zest of 2 lemons
1 cup caster sugar

1 Preheat oven to 165°C.

Base

2 Combine crumbs, butter and sugar. Line four 10cm springform tins with baking paper, then press mixture evenly onto bottoms of tins.

3 Bake for 5 minutes.

Filling

4 Combine cream cheese, juice, zest and sugar in an electric mixer, mix on medium speed until well combined. Add the eggs one at a time, mixing well after each addition. Stir through the currants, then pour filling over the base.

5 Bake for 25 minutes.

Topping

6 Meanwhile, place the lemon zest in a small saucepan and cover with water. Bring to the boil and simmer for 5 minutes. Drain and rinse the zest. In a small saucepan, combine half the sugar with ½ cup water and bring to the boil, add the zest and simmer for 10 minutes. Meanwhile, place the remaining sugar on a tray. Remove zest from the sugar syrup, strain and dry on absorbent paper. Cool slightly, then roll in the tray of sugar until well coated.

7 Once cooled, remove the cheesecakes from the tins, dust with icing sugar and top with the candied lemon zest.

Serves 4

Blackberry Cheesecake

Base

150g digestive biscuits,
finely crushed

¼ cup sugar

1 tablespoon ground cinnamon

50g butter, melted

Filling

750g cream cheese, softened

4 eggs

1 cup sugar

1¼ cups sour cream

3 tablespoons sugar

1 teaspoon vanilla extract

Topping

125g blackberry jam

125g blackberries

1 Preheat oven to 150°C.

Base

2 Combine crumbs, sugar, cinnamon and butter. Press onto bottom of 23cm springform tin.

Filling

3 Whip cream cheese. Add eggs one at a time, whipping after each addition. Gradually add sugar and whip. Pour over base, then bake for 45 minutes.

4 Whip sour cream, sugar and vanilla. Pour on top of baked cheesecake and bake for 10 more minutes. Remove and chill for at least 6 hours.

Topping

5 Heat blackberry jam and blackberries. Cool, then spread over cheesecake. Refrigerate until ready to serve, then let stand at room temperature for 10 minutes before cutting.

12 Slices

Almond Praline Cheesecake

Base

90g digestive biscuits, finely crushed

½ cup slivered almonds, toasted and finely chopped

¼ cup brown sugar, firmly packed

50g unsalted butter, melted

Filling

750g cream cheese, softened

400g canned condensed milk

3 eggs

1 teaspoon almond extract

Topping

⅓ cup dark brown sugar, firmly packed

⅓ cup thickened cream

½ cup slivered almonds, toasted and chopped

1 Preheat oven to 220°C.

Base

2 Combine crumbs, nuts, sugar and butter. Line a 23cm springform tin with baking paper and press crumb mixture onto the bottom.

Filling

3 In a large mixer bowl, beat cream cheese until fluffy. Gradually beat in condensed milk until smooth. Add eggs one at a time, mixing well after each addition, then add almond extract.

4 Pour into tin. Bake for 10 minutes, reduce heat to 150°C and bake for a further 30 minutes.

Topping

5 Meanwhile, combine sugar and cream in a small saucepan. Cook and stir until sugar dissolves, then simmer 5 minutes or until thickened. Remove from heat, stir in almonds.

6 Top cheesecake with almond praline topping and chill before serving.

12 Slices

Cheesecake Brûlée

Base

60g digestive biscuits, finely crushed
¼ cup sugar
30g butter, melted

Filling

500g cream cheese, softened
¼ cup sugar
1 tablespoon lemon juice
zest of 1 small lemon
1 teaspoon vanilla extract
2 large eggs
4 tablespoons caster sugar

1 Preheat oven to 165°C.

Base

2 Combine crumbs, sugar and butter. Line four 10cm springform tins with baking paper, then press mixture evenly onto bottoms of tins.

3 Bake for 5 minutes.

Filling

4 Combine cream cheese, sugar, juice, zest and vanilla in an electric mixer, mix on medium speed until well blended.

5 Beat in eggs one at a time, mixing thoroughly after each addition. Pour over base, then bake for 25 minutes. Cool before removing from tin. Chill.

6 Remove from refrigerator and sprinkle evenly with the caster sugar. Using a blow torch, scorch the tops of the cheesecakes and serve.

Serves 4

German Cheesecake

Base

2 cups plain flour
½ cup sugar
1 teaspoon baking powder
60g butter
1 large egg

Filling

750g cottage cheese
½ cup cornflour
1 teaspoon baking powder
1 cup sugar
4 large eggs
zest of ½ small lemon
½ teaspoon vanilla extract
1 cup sour cream
1 cup raisins

1 Preheat oven to 190°C.

Base

2 In a large mixing bowl, blend together flour, sugar and baking powder. Cut in butter. Add egg and knead until well mixed. Divide the dough in half and use one half to line the bottom of a greased 23cm springform tin, the other half to line the sides. Chill.

Filling

3 Press cottage cheese through a sieve. Combine cornflour and baking powder, set aside. In a large mixing bowl, combine the cottage cheese, sugar, eggs, lemon zest and vanilla. Beat until smooth. Add the cornflour mixture and blend well. Stir in sour cream and raisins. Pour the filling into the prepared base.

4 Bake for 1 hour, or until done – the centre will remain soft. Turn off the oven and, with the door ajar, allow the cake to cool to room temperature.

12 Slices

Italian Cheesecake

Base

150g digestive biscuits, finely crushed

50g butter, melted

Filling

750g ricotta cheese

250g cream cheese

½ cup sugar

2 tablespoons brandy

2 tablespoons vanilla extract

3 large egg yolks

1 Preheat oven to 175°C.

Base

2 Mix together the biscuit crumbs and butter and press into a 23cm springform tin lined with baking paper.

Filling

3 In a large mixing bowl, beat together the ricotta and cream cheese until smooth.

4 Add sugar, brandy and vanilla, mix well. Add the egg yolks and beat until well blended. Pour into base.

5 Bake for 30 minutes, or until the centre is set.

12 Slices

Tropical
Cheesecakes

The tropics are home to a stunning array of delicious
and sometimes unusual fruit, and many of these make
for fabulous cheesecakes, such as guava, papaya
and the unique durian. Mango, passionfruit, banana
and coconut are all readily available and also play
a leading role in many of these cheesecakes.

Guava Strawberry Cheesecake

Base

125g plain flour
60g butter
1 egg yolk
3 tablespoons lemon juice

Filling

250g ricotta cheese
½ cup natural yoghurt
2 eggs
2 tablespoons lemon juice
60g sugar
250g strawberries, sliced
100g guava jam

Base

1 Sift the flour into a bowl. Rub in the butter. Add the egg yolk and lemon juice, with a little cold water if required, to make a soft dough. Knead on a lightly floured surface until smooth, then press the dough evenly over the bottom of a 23cm springform tin. Rest in the refrigerator for 30 minutes.

2 Preheat oven to 190°C. Cover loosely with baking paper and dried beans. Bake blind for 10 minutes, remove the paper and beans and return the pastry base to the oven for 5 minutes more. Cool. Reduce the oven temperature to 180°C.

Filling

3 Beat the ricotta, yoghurt, eggs, lemon juice and sugar in a bowl until smooth. Pour over the pastry base. Bake for 30 minutes or until set, then cool.

4 Purée 100g of the strawberries in a blender or food processor with the guava jam. Spread over the cheesecake. Place in the refrigerator for 1 hour. Decorate with the remaining strawberries to serve.

12 Slices

Cheesecake Sedap

Base
200g shortbread biscuits
25g shredded coconut

Filling
500g cream cheese
250g ricotta cheese
1 cup sugar
1 vanilla bean, split lengthwise
4 large eggs
¼ cup very strong black tea
½ cup shredded coconut, lightly toasted
10–12 fresh lychees

1 Preheat oven to 160°C.

Base

2 Finely grind biscuits in a food processor. Mix together with the coconut, press onto bottom of a lined 23cm springform tin.

3 Bake until crisp, about 10 minutes. Cool on rack while preparing filling.

Filling

4 Using an electric mixer, beat together cream cheese, ricotta and sugar until smooth. Scrape in seeds from vanilla bean, then beat in eggs one at a time until just blended. Beat in the tea, then pour filling over base.

5 Bake until filling is just set and puffed around edges, about 45 minutes.

6 Cool, then release tin sides. Sprinkle toasted coconut around top edge of cake. Top with fresh lychees and serve.

makes 12

Mango Cheesecake

Base

90g butter

250g digestive biscuits, finely crushed

Filling

200g cream cheese

50g sugar

2 mangoes

1½ tablespoons gelatine

⅔ cup thickened cream, whipped

Base

1 Melt the butter and stir in the biscuit crumbs. Press into the base of a lined 20cm springform tin. Chill until firm.

Filling

2 Place the cream cheese and sugar in a bowl and beat together.

3 Peel, stone and purée 1 mango, add to the cheese and sugar and mix well.

4 Dissolve the gelatine in ¼ cup warm water, add to the mango mixture, then add the cream.

5 Mix well, spoon into the cake tin and smooth the surface. Place in refrigerator until set.

6 Chop the remaining mango to decorate the cheesecake and serve with extra whipped cream.

12 Slices

Mini Passionfruit Cheesecake

Base

60g digestive biscuits,
finely crushed

30g butter, melted

¼ cup sugar

Filling

500g cream cheese, softened

¼ cup passionfruit pulp, strained

1 teaspoon vanilla extract

¼ cup sugar

2 large eggs

4 fresh passionfruit

1 Preheat oven to 165°C.

Base

2 Combine crumbs, butter and sugar. Line four 10cm springform tins with baking paper, then press mixture evenly onto bottoms of tins.

3 Bake for 5 minutes.

Filling

4 Combine cream cheese, passionfruit pulp, vanilla and sugar in an electric mixer, mix on medium speed until well combined. Add the eggs one at a time, mixing well after each addition. Divide filling evenly between the bases.

5 Bake for 25 minutes. Cool before removing from tins.

6 Decorate with fresh passionfruit and serve.

Serves 4

Coconut Mango Cheesecake

Base
180g digestive biscuits, finely crushed

1½ cups desiccated coconut, toasted

¼ cup sugar

90g butter, melted

Filling
1kg cream cheese, softened

¾ cup sugar

3 large whole eggs

1 large egg yolk

400mL coconut cream

1 cup thickened cream

1 cup desiccated coconut

½ fresh mango

1 Preheat oven to 165°C.

Base

2 Wrap outside of 23cm springform tin with foil. Mix biscuit crumbs, coconut and sugar in a medium bowl. Add butter and mix. Press mixture onto bottom and up sides of prepared tin. Chill while preparing filling.

Filling

3 Beat cream cheese and sugar in a large bowl until blended. Add whole eggs one at a time, beating after each addition. Beat in egg yolk. Add coconut cream, thickened cream and coconut, beat until just blended. Pour into base.

4 Bake until puffed and golden, about 1 hour and 25 minutes. Transfer to a rack, cool completely. Refrigerate until well chilled.

5 Using a small knife, cut around cheesecake to loosen. Remove tin sides.

6 Purée mango in blender until smooth. Transfer to a small bowl, sweeten with sugar if necessary. Serve cheesecake with mango purée.

12 Slices

Durian Cheesecake

Base

150g butter, melted

125g chocolate cream-filled biscuits, finely crushed

125g digestive biscuits, finely crushed

Filling

1 tablespoon gelatine

250g cream cheese

70g caster sugar

250g durian flesh

½ cup plain yoghurt

¾ cup thickened cream

Base

1 Wrap the base of an 18 x 18cm cake tin with aluminium foil.

2 Slowly drizzle the melted butter into the biscuit crumbs, stirring until almost combined (you might not need to use all the butter). Press into cake tin and chill in refrigerator until firm, about 30 minutes.

Filling

3 Add the gelatine to 2½ tablespoons warm water, dissolve and set aside.

4 Beat the cream cheese and sugar until creamy and light, then add the durian and continue to beat until well combined.

5 Pour in the gelatine mixture and yoghurt, stir until combined.

6 Add the cream and slowly stir until the mixture is creamy and well mixed.

7 Pour the filling into the tin and chill for at least 3 hours or overnight.

8 Slices

Banana Cheesecake

Base

120g digestive biscuits, finely crushed
⅓ cup linseed meal
60g butter, melted

Filling

500g cream cheese
2 medium bananas, mashed
2 cups sour cream
1 cup sugar
3 eggs
1 tablespoon cornflour
3 tablespoons lemon juice
1½ teaspoons vanilla extract

1 Preheat oven to 180°C.

Base

2 Thoroughly mix biscuit crumbs, linseed meal and butter. Spread onto bottom of a lined 23cm springform tin. Cook for 10 minutes.

Filling

3 Beat the cream cheese until soft and smooth, add the banana, sour cream and sugar and beat until smooth. Add the eggs one at a time, mixing thoroughly after each addition. Add the cornflour, lemon juice and vanilla. Mix thoroughly, pour into base. Bake for 1 hour. Turn off the oven and leave cheesecake in for another hour.

4 Top with whipped cream and roasted hazelnuts to serve.

12 Slices

Passionfruit and Lychee Cheesecake

Base

60g digestive biscuits, finely crushed

¼ cup sugar

30g butter, melted

Filling

500g cream cheese, softened

¼ cup passionfruit pulp, strained

¼ cup sugar

2 large eggs

8 lychees

1 Preheat oven to 165°C.

Base

2 Combine crumbs, sugar and butter. Line four 10cm springform tins with baking paper, then press mixture evenly onto bottoms of tins.

3 Bake for 5 minutes.

Filling

4 Combine cream cheese, pulp and sugar in an electric mixer, mix on medium speed until well blended. Beat in eggs one at a time, mixing thoroughly after each addition. Divide filling evenly between bases.

5 Bake for 25 minutes.

6 Cool the cheesecakes before removing from the tins.

7 Decorate with extra pulp and lychees.

Serves 4

Banana Brazil Nut Cheesecake

Base

120g digestive biscuits, finely crushed

60g Brazil nuts, ground

50g butter, melted

Filling

1 vanilla pod, split in half lengthwise

500g cream cheese

2 medium bananas, mashed

2 cups sour cream

1 cup sugar

3 eggs

40g Brazil nuts, ground

1 tablespoon banana liqueur

1 tablespoon cornflour

3 tablespoons lime juice

1 Preheat oven to 180°C.

Base

2 Thoroughly mix biscuit crumbs, Brazil nuts and butter. Spread onto bottom of 23cm springform tin. Bake for 10 minutes.

Filling

3 Scrape the vanilla seeds from the pod and discard the pod. Beat the cream cheese until soft and smooth, add the bananas, sour cream and sugar and beat until smooth. Add the eggs one at a time, mixing thoroughly after each addition. Add the Brazil nuts, liqueur, cornflour, lime juice and vanilla seeds. Mix thoroughly, then pour filling into base.

4 Bake for 1 hour. Turn off the oven and leave cheesecake in for another hour.

5 Serve topped with whipped cream and extra Brazil nuts.

12 Slices

Jamaican Rice Cheesecake

Base

60g digestive biscuits,
finely crushed

1 cup finely chopped almonds

¼ cup sugar

50g butter, melted

Filling

2 cups cooked rice

1½ cups sour cream

90g butter, melted

500g ricotta cheese

500g cream cheese, softened

1½ cups sugar

4 large eggs

¼ cup rum

1 teaspoon vanilla extract

Topping

¾ cup sour cream

2 tablespoons sugar

½ teaspoon vanilla extract

1 Preheat oven to 180°C.

Base

2 Combine biscuit crumbs, almonds, sugar and butter in a medium mixing bowl. Press into bottom and 25mm up sides of an ungreased 23cm springform tin.

Filling

3 Combine rice, sour cream and butter in food processor or blender, process until well blended and set aside.

4 Beat ricotta, cream cheese and sugar in a large mixing bowl until light and fluffy. Add eggs one at a time, beating well after each addition. Blend in rum, vanilla and rice mixture.

5 Pour filling into prepared base. Bake for 1 hour. Turn oven off and leave cheesecake in oven an additional 2 hours. Cool. Refrigerate at least 8 hours or overnight.

Topping

6 Combine sour cream, sugar and vanilla, spread over cheesecake. Decorate with fresh tropical fruit and shredded coconut.

Serves 12

Boa Vista Cheesecake

Base
¾ cup instant polenta
50g vanilla wafers, finely crushed
50g butter, melted

Filling
500g cream cheese, softened
⅓ cup glucose
2 tablespoons milk
2 large eggs
½ cup macadamias, toasted and chopped
¼ fresh pineapple, diced
½ fresh papaya, diced
passionfruit pulp

1 Preheat oven to 175°C.

Base

2 Combine polenta, crumbs and butter, press onto bottom of a lined 23cm springform tin. Bake for 10 minutes.

Filling

3 Combine cream cheese, glucose and milk in an electric mixer, mix on medium speed until well blended. Add eggs one at a time, mixing well after each addition. Stir in macadamias, pour over base.

4 Bake for 45 minutes.

5 Loosen cake from rim, cool before removing. Chill.

6 Top with pineapple, papaya and passionfruit and serve.

12 Slices

Cocomoco Cheesecake

Base
120g digestive biscuits, finely crushed
3 tablespoons sugar
50g butter, melted

Filling
60g cooking chocolate
40g butter
500g cream cheese, softened
1¼ cups sugar
5 large eggs
1⅓ cups flaked coconut

Topping
1 cup sour cream
2 tablespoons sugar
2 tablespoons passionfruit liqueur
1 teaspoon instant coffee

1 Preheat oven to 175°C.

Base
2 Combine crumbs, sugar and butter, press onto bottom of 23cm springform tin. Bake for 10 minutes.

Filling
3 Melt chocolate and butter over low heat, stirring until smooth.
4 Combine cream cheese and sugar in an electric mixer, mix on medium speed until well blended. Add eggs one at a time, mixing well after each addition. Blend in chocolate mixture and coconut, pour over base.
5 Bake for 60 minutes or until set.

Topping
6 Combine sour cream, sugar, liqueur and coffee, spread over cheesecake.
7 Reduce heat to 150°C and bake for 5 minutes.
8 Loosen cake from rim of tin, cool before removing. Chill.

12 Slices

Calypso Cheesecake

Base
¾ cup ground almonds
20g butter, melted

Filling
1½ tablespoons gelatine
450g cream cheese
¾ cup milk
¾ cup sugar
2 tablespoons rum

Topping
½ cup sugar
2 tablespoons rum
¼ pineapple, cut into small pieces
toasted shredded coconut

Base

1 Stir together almonds and butter in a small bowl.
2 Line four 10cm springform tins with baking paper, then press mixture evenly onto bottoms of tins.

Filling

3 Soften gelatine in ¼ cup water in a small saucepan, stir over low heat until dissolved. Beat cream cheese, milk, sugar and rum in an electric mixer until well blended. Stir in the gelatine and mix well. Pour into the springform tins, refrigerate for 3 hours or overnight.

Topping

4 Combine the sugar and rum with ¼ cup water in a saucepan, bring to the boil then simmer for 15 minutes. Add the pineapple pieces to the syrup and cool.
5 Divide topping evenly between cheesecakes, then top with coconut.

Serves 4

Papaya Lime Cheesecake

Base

¼ cup sugar

20g butter, softened

330g gingernut biscuits, finely crushed

Filling

180g cottage cheese

250g cream cheese, softened

1 cup sour cream

½ cup sugar

½ cup coconut cream

¼ cup plain flour

1 teaspoon coconut extract

3 eggs

Topping

1½ cups caster sugar

3–4 fresh limes, thinly sliced

¼ papaya, cubed

1   Preheat oven to 175°C.

Base

2   Mix together the sugar, butter and biscuit crumbs in a bowl. Press into a lined 23cm springform tin.

3   Bake for 12 minutes, cool on a wire rack. Lower heat to 150°C.

Filling

4   Place cheeses in a food processor, process for 2 minutes or until smooth, scraping sides of processor bowl once. Add sour cream, sugar, coconut cream, flour, coconut extract and eggs, process for 20 seconds, scraping sides of processor bowl once.

5   Pour cheese mixture into base, bake for 1½ hours or until almost set. Turn oven off, and let cheesecake stand for 1 hour in oven with door closed. Remove cheesecake from oven, cover and chill for 1 hour.

Topping

6   Place 1 cup water and 1 cup of sugar in a pan. Bring to the boil and simmer until sugar dissolves. Add the lime slices and simmer for 10 minutes. Meanwhile, place the remaining sugar on a tray.

7   Remove the lime slices from the heat, strain and dry on absorbent paper. Cool slightly, then place one at a time on the tray of sugar to coat. Decorate the cheesecake with the lime slices and papaya.

12 Slices

Eastern Cheesecakes

Perhaps less well known than other cheesecakes, those of the East are often subtly flavoured with exotic spices and fruits, and may also feature tantalising toppings for the perfect finish. While some of the ingredients may be a little harder to find than normal, don't let that put you off – your tastebuds will reward you for the extra effort.

Yoghurt Cheesecake

Base

180g digestive biscuits, finely crushed

1 teaspoon ground cinnamon

½ teaspoon ground cardamom

2 tablespoons sugar

90g butter, melted

Filling

2 tablespoons gelatine

250g kashta cheese

250g cottage cheese

1 cup yoghurt

3 eggs, separated

1¼ cups sugar

pinch of salt

zest of 1 large lemon

2 tablespoons lemon juice

1 cup thickened cream

50g Persian fairy floss

Base

1 Mix together the biscuit crumbs, cinnamom, cardamom, sugar and butter. Firmly press onto the bottom of a 23cm springform tin. Chill until ready to use.

Filling

2 Dissolve the gelatine in ¼ cup warm water.

3 Beat together the kashta, cottage cheese and yoghurt. Set aside.

4 In a double boiler, beat the egg yolks with ¾ cup of the sugar, the salt and lemon zest. Put over simmering water and cook, stirring constantly for 5 minutes.

5 Add the gelatine and stir until well combined. Remove from heat and cool slightly.

6 Stir in the cheese mixture and the lemon juice.

7 Beat the egg whites until they form soft peaks, add the remaining sugar, and continue beating until stiff. Fold into the cheese mixture. Whip the cream and fold in.

8 Pour the filling into the prepared base and chill for 8 hours or overnight.

9 Decorate with Persian fairy floss and serve.

12 Slices

Note: Kashta is a heavy cream style of fresh cheese. Ask for it in local Lebanese and Middle Eastern supermarkets.

Orange, Cardamom and Lime Cheesecake

Base
150g plain sweet biscuits, finely crushed
90g butter, melted

Filling
200g cream cheese, softened
½ teaspoon ground cardamom
2 tablespoons brown sugar
zest of 1 orange
zest of 2 limes
3 teaspoons orange juice
3 teaspoons lime juice
1 egg, lightly beaten
½ cup condensed milk
2 tablespoons thickened cream, whipped

1 Preheat oven to 180°C.

Base

2 Combine biscuits and butter in a bowl and mix to combine. Press biscuit mixture over base and sides of a well-oiled 23cm springform tin. Bake for 5–8 minutes, then remove from oven and set aside to cool.

Filling

3 Place cream cheese, cardamom, sugar, orange and lime zest, and orange and lime juice in a mixing bowl and beat until creamy. Beat in egg, then mix in condensed milk and fold in cream.

4 Spoon mixture into prepared base and bake for 25–30 minutes or until just firm. Turn oven off and allow cheesecake to cool in oven with door ajar. Chill before serving.

5 Serve decorated with toasted coconut.

12 Slices

Lemon Sultana Cheesecake

Base

½ cup plain flour

¼ cup cornflour

¼ cup custard powder

1 tablespoon icing sugar

60g butter

1 egg yolk

⅓ cup caster sugar

1 tablespoon ground cinnamom

1 tablespoon ground cardamom

Filling

375g cream cheese, softened

¼ cup natural yoghurt

½ cup caster sugar

2 eggs

1 teaspoon vanilla extract

zest of 1 lemon

170g sultanas

Topping

½ cup double cream

2 teaspoons lemon juice

zest of ½ lemon

1 Preheat oven to 180°C.

Base

2 Sift flour, cornflour, custard powder and icing sugar into a large mixing bowl. Rub in butter with your fingers until mixture resembles coarse breadcrumbs. Make a well in the centre of the mixture and stir in egg yolk and enough iced water to make a firm dough. Wrap in cling wrap and refrigerate for 30 minutes.

3 Roll out pastry to fit the base of a greased 20cm springform tin. Using a fork, prick pastry base and bake for 10 minutes. Set aside to cool.

4 In a bowl mix together the sugar, cinnamon and cardamom. Spread evenly over cooled pastry base.

Filling

5 Place cream cheese, yoghurt, sugar, eggs, vanilla extract and lemon zest in a mixing bowl and beat until smooth. Fold in sultanas.

6 Spoon mixture into prepared base. Reduce oven temperature to 180°C and bake for 20–25 minutes or until firm. Turn off oven and leave cheesecake to cool in oven with door ajar.

Topping

7 Place cream, lemon juice and zest in a small saucepan and bring to a boil, then simmer, stirring, for 5 minutes or until mixture thickens. Pour topping over cooled cheesecake and chill until required.

12 Slices

Ginger Honey Cheesecake

Base

250g gingernut biscuits, finely crushed

1 tablespoon sugar

50g butter, chilled

Filling

500g cream cheese, softened

½ cup honey

½ cup sugar

2 large eggs, at room temperature

300g kashta cheese

1 tablespoon lemon juice

1½ teaspoons vanilla extract

¾ cup dates, very finely chopped

2 tablespoons glacé ginger, very finely chopped

1 Preheat oven to 180°C.

Base

2 Butter only the sides of a 23cm springform tin. Mix the crumbs and sugar in a bowl. Add the butter and rub it in well with your fingers. Distribute the crumbs loosely but evenly in the pan and push them slightly up the sides. Cover and chill while you make the filling.

Filling

3 Using an electric mixer, cream the cream cheese, honey and sugar until light and fluffy. Beat in the eggs one at a time, then add the remaining ingredients and continue to beat until evenly blended. Pour the filling into the tin and bake for 1 hour and 15 minutes. Cool thoroughly on a rack, then cover, still in the tin, and refrigerate for 12 hours before removing from the tin and slicing.

4 Dust the cheesecake with icing sugar before serving.

12 Slices

Note: Kashta is a heavy cream style of fresh cheese. Ask for it in local Lebanese and Middle Eastern supermarkets.

Kashta Cheesecake

Base

1 cup semolina
2 tablespoons icing sugar
zest of 1 lemon
1 teaspoon ground cinnamon
¼ teaspoon nutmeg
100g butter, chopped

Filling

650g cream cheese, softened
250g kashta cheese
1½ cups sugar
6 large eggs, separated
juice and zest of 1 large lemon
¾ cup walnuts, ground
50g butter, softened
¾ cup plain flour
1 cup thickened cream
1 cup sultanas

1 Preheat oven to 200°C.

Base

2 Line a 23cm springform tin with baking paper.
3 Mix semolina, sugar, zest and spices together, rub in butter until mixture resembles fine breadcrumbs. Add enough water to make ingredients come together.
4 Press evenly onto the bottom of the tin, line with baking paper, half-fill with dried beans and blind bake for 10 minutes. Remove the paper and beans.

Filling

5 Meanwhile, combine the cream cheese, kashta and 1 cup of sugar in an electric mixer and beat for 4 minutes until smooth. Add the egg yolks one at a time, beating well after each addition. Add the lemon juice and zest, walnuts, butter and flour and mix until combined.
6 In a separate bowl, beat the egg whites until foaming then add the remaining sugar. Beat until thick and glossy.
7 In another bowl, beat the cream until soft peaks form. Fold the cream and egg whites into the cheese mixture, combine thoroughly. Pour into the cooled base and sprinkle over the sultanas.
8 Bake for 10 minutes then reduce heat to 150°C and cook for an hour. Turn off the oven and leave the cake in the oven. When cake has cooled, remove and refrigerate overnight.
9 Dust with icing sugar to serve.

12 Slices

Note: Kashta is a heavy cream style of fresh cheese. Ask for it in local Lebanese and Middle Eastern supermarkets.

Wild Fig and Blood Orange Cheesecake

Base

180g malt biscuits, finely crushed
50g butter, melted

Filling

500g cream cheese
250g ricotta cheese
1 cup sugar
1 vanilla bean, split lengthwise
4 large eggs

Topping

zest of 1 blood orange
juice of 3 blood oranges
½ cup sugar
200g wild figs

1 Preheat oven to 160°C.

Base

2 Mix together the biscuit crumbs and the butter, press into the bottom of a lined 23cm springform tin.

3 Bake for 10 minutes. Cool on rack while preparing filling.

Filling

4 Using an electric mixer, beat together the cream cheese, ricotta and sugar until smooth. Scrape in seeds from vanilla bean. Beat in eggs, one at a time, until just blended. Pour filling over base (mixture will not fill tin). Bake until filling is just set and puffed around edges, about 45 minutes.

Topping

5 Combine 1 cup water with all the topping ingredients except the figs in a saucepan, bring to the boil, add the figs and simmer for 10 minutes. Remove from the heat and soak for 2 hours.

6 Strain the figs, reserving the liquid. Return liquid to the pan and reduce for 5 minutes to a thick syrup.

7 Decorate the top of the cheesecake with figs and syrup.

12 Slices

Spiced Plum Cheesecake

Base
75g butter, melted
75g almond meal
75g sweet biscuits, finely crushed

Filling
825g canned plums in juice, drained
250g kashta cheese
⅓ cup sour cream
⅔ cup caster sugar
1 teaspoon vanilla extract
⅓ cup hot milk
¼ cup cornflour
4 eggs, separated

1 Preheat oven to 210°C.

Base

2 Combine the butter, almond meal and biscuit crumbs in a bowl and mix well. Press into the base of a 25cm springform tin.

Filling

3 Arrange the plums, cut-side down, over the base.

4 Place the kashta, sour cream, ¼ cup of the caster sugar and the vanilla in an electric mixer and beat until smooth. Add the hot milk and beat until smooth, then add the cornflour and egg yolks and mix well.

5 In a clean bowl, whisk the egg whites to firm peaks, then whisk in the remaining sugar to make a firm meringue. Fold into the cheese mixture, then pour over the plum base.

6 Bake for 10 minutes, then reduce the temperature to 160°C and bake for another 1 hour and 20 minutes or until a skewer inserted in the centre of the cake comes out clean.

7 Allow to cool, run a sharp knife around the inside of the tin and remove. Serve dusted with icing sugar.

12 Slices

Note: Kashta is a heavy cream style of fresh cheese. Ask for it in local Lebanese and Middle Eastern supermarkets.

Pistachio and White Mulberry Cheesecake

Base

60g digestive biscuits,
finely crushed

¼ cup sugar

30g butter, melted

Filling

500g cream cheese, softened

¼ cup sugar

1 tablespoon orange juice

zest of ½ orange

1 teaspoon orange blossom water

2 large eggs

Topping

zest of 1 orange

1 tablespoon orange blossom water

½ cup sugar

50g dried white mulberries

30g pistachios

1   Preheat oven to 165°C.

Base

2   Combine crumbs, sugar and butter. Line four 10cm springform tins with baking paper, then press mixture evenly onto bottoms of tins.

3   Bake for 5 minutes.

Filling

4   Combine cream cheese, sugar, juice, zest and orange blossom water in an electric mixer, mix on medium speed until well blended. Beat in eggs one at a time, mixing thoroughly after each addition. Divide filling evenly between each base.

5   Bake for 25 minutes.

Topping

6   Meanwhile, combine the orange zest, orange blossom water, sugar and 1 cup water in a saucepan. Bring to the boil and simmer for 15 minutes. In a bowl, place the mulberries and pistachios, pour over the syrup. Cool.

7   Cool the cheesecakes before removing from the tins.

8   Decorate each cheesecake with some of the mulberries, pistachios and syrup. Serve any remaining topping on a plate.

Serves 4

Bedouin Date Cheesecake

Base
20g butter
1 cup self-raising flour
¼ cup rolled oats
½ teaspoon ground ginger

Filling
225g dates
½ cup unsweetened orange juice
1kg ricotta cheese
4 eggs, lightly beaten
1¼ cups condensed milk
½ cup raisins, chopped
zest of 1 large lemon
2 tablespoons sugar
100g kataifi pastry

1 Preheat oven to 200°C.

Base

2 In a bowl, rub butter into the flour until crumbly. Mix in oats, ginger and enough water to make a stiff, dry dough.

3 Roll out dough to a circle 1cm thick. Carefully press into the base of a 25cm springform tin. Line with baking paper, half-fill with dried beans and blind bake for 10 minutes, remove the paper and beans. Set aside and allow to cool.

Filling

4 Meanwhile, add dates and orange juice to a small saucepan, simmer gently until reduced to a soft paste. Cool.

5 Spread evenly over the base. Chill until ready to serve.

6 Beat together the cheese and eggs, then gradually beat in condensed milk until smooth.

7 Stir in raisins, lemon zest and sugar. Pour the mixture into base and top evenly with kataifi.

8 Bake for 15 minutes. Reduce heat to 190°C and continue baking for 1½ hours or until a skewer inserted in the centre comes out clean. Cool on a wire rack.

12 Slices

Upside-Down Orange and Pomegranate Cheesecake

Base

65g ground almonds

⅓ cup caster sugar

⅓ cup plain flour

⅓ cup butter

Filling

2 cups sugar

3 whole oranges, thinly sliced

500g cream cheese, at room temperature

2 tablespoons Grand Marnier or Cointreau

1 tablespoon lemon juice

1 tablespoon gelatine

1¼ cups thickened cream, whipped

seeds of 1 pomegranate

1 Preheat oven to 160°C.

Base

2 Place the almonds, sugar, flour and butter in a food processor, process until mixture forms a paste. Press into the base of a greased 20cm springform tin and bake for 20–25 minutes. Allow to cool, then turn out.

Filling

3 Place the sugar and 1 cup water together in a large saucepan and bring to the boil. Simmer, stirring until the sugar dissolves, add orange slices and simmer gently for 10–15 minutes. Remove the oranges carefully from the syrup and drain on absorbent paper. Reserve the syrup.

4 Arrange the best orange slices over the base and sides of the tin in an overlapping pattern (remember that the filling will only half-fill the tin). Chop enough of the remaining slices to fill ½ cup.

5 Place the cream cheese in a bowl and beat until smooth, gradually beat in the liqueur, lemon juice and chopped orange.

6 Whisk the gelatine into ½ cup of the hot reserved orange syrup until dissolved, allow to cool. Add the gelatine mixture to the cheese mixture and beat until well mixed.

7 Lightly whip the cream and fold it gently into the cheese mixture. And the pomegranate seeds. Pour the mixture into the prepared tin. Place baked base on top and press down until level. Refrigerate for 3 hours.

8 Place the cheesecake upside down on a serving platter, then remove the mould. Brush top of cheesecake with remaining orange syrup before serving.

12 Slices

Yoghurt, Rose and Date Cheesecake

Base
200g digestive biscuits
75g butter, melted

Filling
½ cup caster sugar
¼ cup fresh orange juice, strained
1½ tablespoons gelatine
1¼ cups thickened cream
500g Greek yoghurt
3 teaspoons rose water
4 large fresh dates, sliced
1 tablespoon honey

Base
1 Line the base and sides of a 23cm springform tin with baking paper.
2 Place the biscuits in a food processor and process until finely crushed. Add the butter and process until combined. Transfer to the lined tin, press the mixture firmly over the base. Place in the refrigerator for 30 minutes.

Filling
3 Meanwhile, place the caster sugar and orange juice in a saucepan over low heat. Stir until the sugar dissolves.
4 Combine 2 tablespoons water and the gelatine in a small saucepan, stir over low heat until dissolved. Add the gelatine mixture to the orange juice mixture.
5 Beat the cream until soft peaks form.
6 Place the yoghurt in a large bowl, beat in the rose water, then the orange juice mixture. Use a metal spoon to fold in cream. Pour filling over the base. Top with slices of fresh date and drizzle with honey. Cover with a large plate and refrigerate overnight to set.

12 Slices

Pumpkin, Fig and Raisin Cheesecake

Base
1 cup semolina
2 tablespoons icing sugar
zest of ½ lemon
100g butter, chopped

Filling
1 medium lime
½ cup caster sugar
2 cinnamon sticks
150g dried figs
100g pumpkin, mashed and cooled
180g kashta cheese
2 teaspoons cornflour
3 egg yolks
¾ cup thickened cream
¼ cup raisins
zest of ½ lemon
1 tablespoon dark rum

1 Preheat oven to 180°C.

Base

2 Grease a 23cm springform tin. Mix semolina, sugar and lemon zest, rub in butter until mixture resembles fine breadcrumbs. Add enough water to make ingredients come together.

3 Press evenly into prepared tin. Bake for 15 minutes or until lightly browned. Allow to cool.

Filling

4 Remove zest from lime, combine with 1½ tablespoons of the sugar, 1½ cups water and the cinnamon in a medium saucepan, stir over heat until sugar is dissolved. Bring to the boil, add figs and simmer uncovered for 5 minutes. Remove from heat, stand for 3 hours.

5 Preheat oven to 180°C. Remove figs from syrup, pat dry and finely chop. Whisk pumpkin, cheese, cornflour, remaining sugar and egg yolks in a bowl until combined. Add chopped figs, cream, raisins, lemon zest and rum, mix well.

6 Pour filling over base, bake for 50 minutes or until the centre of the cheesecake is almost set. Turn oven off, cool cheesecake in oven with door ajar.

12 Slices

Note: Kashta is a heavy cream style of fresh cheese. Ask for it in local Lebanese and Middle Eastern supermarkets.

Turkish Delight Cheesecake

Base
¾ cup ground almonds
20g butter, melted

Filling
1½ tablespoons gelatine
450g cream cheese
¾ cup milk
¾ cup sugar
2 tablespoons rose water
16 pieces Turkish delight

Base

1 Stir together almonds and butter in a small bowl.
2 Line four 10cm springform tins with baking paper, then press mixture evenly onto bottoms of tins.

Filling

3 Soften gelatine in ¼ cup water in small saucepan, stir over low heat until dissolved. Beat cream cheese, milk, sugar and rose water with an electric mixer until well blended.
4 Divide filling evenly between each base, place in the refrigerator for 3 hours or overnight.
5 Decorate with Turkish delight and serve.

Serves 4

Plum and Bitter Orange Cheesecake

Base
150g gingernut biscuits
80g butter, melted

Filling
825g canned plums in juice
500g cream cheese, softened
½ cup sour cream
zest of ½ orange
1 tablespoon orange juice
2–3 drops Angostura bitters
3 eggs
¾ cup caster sugar
2 tablespoons plain flour
2 tablespoons flaked almonds

Topping
¼ cup caster sugar
¼ cup unsweetened orange juice
zest of 1 orange
3–4 drops Angostura bitters
½ cup cream
2 teaspoons ground cinnamon

1 Preheat oven to 150°C.

Base
2 Line base of a 23cm springform tin with baking paper.
3 In a food processor, process the biscuits until finely crushed, transfer to a bowl and stir in the melted butter until combined. Press firmly over the base of the tin, refrigerate while preparing filling.

Filling
4 Drain the plums, reserving the liquid. Halve the plums and remove the stones.
5 Combine the remaining filling ingredients, except the almonds, in a large bowl. Beat with an electric mixer for about 5 minutes or until thick and smooth.
6 Pour filling over the base, top with the plums and sprinkle with almonds. Bake, uncovered, for 1 hour or until set. Cool in the tin.

Topping
7 Place the reserved plum juice, sugar, orange juice, zest and bitters into a small saucepan, bring to the boil, then simmer, uncovered, until reduced by half. Allow to cool.
8 Combine cream and cinnamon in a bowl and whisk to firm peaks.
9 Serve the cheesecake topped with the plum syrup and cinnamon cream.

12 Slices

Glossary

Acidulated water: water with added acid, such as lemon juice or vinegar, which prevents discolouration of ingredients, particularly fruit or vegetables. The proportion of acid to water is 1 teaspoon per 300mL.

Al dente: Italian cooking term for ingredients that are cooked until tender but still firm to the bite; usually applied to pasta.

Américaine: method of serving seafood, usually lobster and monkfish, in a sauce flavoured with olive oil, aromatic herbs, tomatoes, white wine, fish stock, brandy and tarragon.

Anglaise: cooking style for simple cooked dishes such as boiled vegetables. Assiette anglaise is a plate of cold cooked meats.

Antipasto: Italian for 'before the meal', it denotes an assortment of cold meats, vegetables and cheeses, often marinated, served as an hors d'oeuvre. A typical antipasto might include salami, prosciutto, marinated artichoke hearts, anchovy fillets, olives, tuna and provolone cheese.

Au gratin: food sprinkled with breadcrumbs, often covered with cheese sauce and browned until a crisp coating forms.

Bain marie: a saucepan standing in a large pan which is filled with boiling water to keep liquids at simmering point. A double boiler will do the same job.

Balsamic vinegar: a mild, extremely fragrant, wine-based vinegar made in northern Italy. Traditionally, the vinegar is aged for at least seven years in a series of casks made of various woods.

Baste: to moisten food while it is cooking by spooning or brushing on liquid or fat.

Beat: to stir thoroughly and vigorously.

Beurre manie: equal quantities of butter and flour kneaded together and added, a little at a time, to thicken a stew or casserole.

Bird: see *paupiette*.

Blanc: a cooking liquid made by adding flour and lemon juice to water in order to keep certain vegetables from discolouring as they cook.

Blanch: to plunge into boiling water and then, in some cases, into cold water. Fruits and nuts are blanched to remove skin easily.

Blanquette: a white stew of lamb, veal or chicken, bound with egg yolks and cream and accompanied by onion and mushrooms.

Blend: to mix thoroughly.

Bonne femme: dishes cooked in the traditional French 'housewife' style. Chicken and pork *bonne femme* are garnished with bacon, potatoes and baby onion; fish *bonne femme* with mushrooms in a white-wine sauce.

Bouquet garni: a bunch of herbs, usually consisting of sprigs of parsley, thyme, marjoram, rosemary, a bay leaf, peppercorns and cloves, tied in muslin and used to flavour stews and casseroles.

Braise: to cook whole or large pieces of poultry, game, fish, meat or vegetables in a small amount of wine, stock or other liquid in a closed pot. Often the main ingredient is first browned in fat and then cooked in a low oven or very slowly on top of the stove. Braising suits tough meats and older birds and produces a mellow, rich sauce.

Broil: the American term for grilling food.

Brown: cook in a small amount of fat until brown.

Burghul (also bulgur): a type of cracked wheat, where the kernels are steamed and dried before being crushed.

Buttered: to spread with softened or melted butter.

Butterfly: to slit a piece of food in half horizontally, cutting it almost through so that when opened it resembles butterfly wings. Chops, large prawns and thick fish fillets are often butterflied so that they cook more quickly and evenly.

Buttermilk: a tangy, low-fat cultured milk product; its slight acidity makes it an ideal marinade base for poultry.

Calzone: a semicircular pocket of pizza dough, stuffed with meat or vegetables, sealed and baked.

Caramelise: to melt sugar until it is a golden-brown syrup.

Chai (also known as masala chai): middle Eastern and Asian word for tea. Typically spiced with cardamom, cinnamon, ginger, star anise, peppercorns and cloves.

Champignons: small mushrooms, usually canned.

Chasseur: French for 'hunter'; a French cooking style in which meat and chicken dishes are cooked with mushrooms, spring onions, white wine and often tomato.

Clarify: to melt butter and drain the oil off the sediment.

Coat: to cover with a thin layer of flour, sugar, nuts, crumbs, poppy or sesame seeds, cinnamon sugar or a few of the ground spices.

Concasser: to chop coarsely, usually tomatoes.

Confit: from the French verb *confire*, meaning to preserve, food that is made into a preserve by cooking very slowly and thoroughly until tender. In the case of meat, such as duck or goose, it is cooked in its own fat, and covered with the fat so that the meat does not come into contact with the air. Vegetables such as onions are good in confit.

Consommé: a clear soup usually made from beef.

Coulis: a thin purée, usually of fresh or cooked fruit or vegetables, which is soft enough to pour (in French *couler* means 'to run'). A coulis may be rough-textured or very smooth.

Court bouillon: the liquid in which fish, poultry or meat is cooked. It usually consists of water with bay leaf, onion, carrots and salt and freshly ground black pepper to taste. Other additives may include wine, vinegar, stock, garlic or spring onions.

Couscous: cereal processed from semolina into pellets, traditionally steamed and served with meat and vegetables in the classic North African stew of the same name.

Cream: to make soft, smooth and creamy by rubbing with the back of a spoon or by beating with a mixer. Usually applied to fat and sugar.

Croutons: small toasted or fried cubes of bread.

Cruciferous vegetables: certain members of the mustard, cabbage and turnip families with cross-shaped flowers and strong aromas and flavours.

Crudités: raw vegetables, cut in slices or sticks to nibble plain or with a dipping sauce, or shredded vegetables tossed as salad with a simple dressing.

Cube: to cut into small pieces with six equal sides.

Curdle: to cause milk or sauce to separate into solid and liquid. Example, overcooked egg mixtures.

Daikon radish (also called mooli): a long white Japanese radish.

Dark sesame oil (also called Oriental sesame oil): dark polyunsaturated oil with a low burning point, used for seasoning. Do not replace with lighter sesame oil.

Deglaze: to dissolve congealed cooking juices or glaze on the bottom of a pan by adding a liquid, then scraping and stirring vigorously whilst bringing the liquid to the boil. Juices may be used to make gravy or to add to sauce.

Degrease: to skim grease from the surface of liquid. If possible the liquid should be chilled so the fat solidifies. If not, skim off most of the fat with a large metal spoon, then trail strips of paper towel on the surface of the liquid to remove any remaining globules.

Devilled: a dish or sauce that is highly seasoned with a hot ingredient such as mustard, Worcestershire sauce or cayenne pepper.

Dice: to cut into small cubes.

Dietary fibre: a plant-cell material that is undigested or only partially digested in the human body, but which promotes healthy digestion of other food matter.

Dissolve: mix a dry ingredient with liquid until absorbed.

Double boiler: a large pot of water is brought to the boil and a smaller pot is placed into the larger pot. Cooking then takes place in the smaller pot at a constant 100°C.

Dredge: to coat with a dry ingredient, such as flour or sugar.

Drizzle: to pour in a fine thread-like stream over a surface.

Dust: to sprinkle or coat lightly with flour or icing sugar.

Dutch oven: a heavy casserole with a lid usually made from cast iron or pottery.

Emulsion: a mixture of two liquids that are not mutually soluble; for example, oil and water.

Entrée: in Europe, the 'entry' or hors d'oeuvre; in North America entree means the main course.

Fenugreek: a small, slender annual herb of the pea family. The seeds are spice. Ground fenugreek has a strong maple sweetness, spicy but bitter flavour and an aroma of burnt sugar.

Fillet: special cut of beef, lamb, pork or veal; breast of poultry and game; fish cut off the bone lengthwise.

Flake: to break into small pieces with a fork.

Flame: to ignite warmed alcohol over food.

Fold in: a gentle, careful combining of a light or delicate mixture with a heavier mixture, using a metal spoon.

Fondant: a sweet icing used for filling or topping cakes. Comprising of sugar, glucose and water boiled, cooled and beaten to form an opaque creamy consistency.

Frenched: when fat and gristle is scraped and cut from meat on a bone, leaving the meaty part virtually fat free.

Fricassé: a dish in which poultry, fish or vegetables are bound together with a white or velouté sauce. In Britain and the United States, the name applies to an old-fashioned dish of chicken in a creamy sauce.

Galangal: A member of the ginger family, commonly known as Lao or Siamese ginger. It has a peppery taste with overtones of ginger.

Galette: sweet or savoury mixture shaped as a flat round.

Ganache: a filling or glaze made of full cream, chocolate, and/or other flavourings, often used to sandwich the layers of gourmet chocolate cakes

Garnish: to decorate food, usually with something edible.

Gastrique: caramelised sugar deglazed with vinegar and used in fruit-flavoured savoury sauces, in such dishes as duck with orange.

Ghee: butter, clarified by boiling. Commonly used in Indian cooking.

Glaze: a thin coating of beaten egg, syrup or aspic which is brushed over pastry, fruits or cooked meats.

Gluten: a protein in flour that is developed when dough is kneaded, making the dough elastic.

Gratin: a dish cooked in the oven or under the grill so that it develops a brown crust. Breadcrumbs or cheese may be sprinkled on top first. Shallow gratin dishes ensure a maximum area of crust.

Grease: to rub or brush lightly with oil or fat.

Infuse: to immerse herbs, spices or other flavourings in hot liquid to flavour it. Infusion takes 2–5 minutes depending on the flavouring. The liquid should be very hot but not boiling.

Jardinière: a garnish of garden vegetables, typically carrots, pickling onions, French beans and turnips.

Joint: to cut poultry, game or small animals into serving pieces by dividing at the joint.

Julienne: to cut food into match-like strips.

Lights: lungs of an animal, used in various meat preparations such as pâtés and faggots.

Line: to cover the inside of a container with paper, to protect or aid in removing mixture.

Knead: to work dough using heel of hand with a pressing motion, while stretching and folding the dough.

Macerate: to soak food in liquid to soften.

Marinade: a seasoned liquid, usually an oil and acid mixture, in which meats or other foods are soaked to soften and give more flavour.

Marinara: Italian 'sailor's style' cooking that does not apply to any particular combination of ingredients. Marinara tomato sauce for pasta is the most familiar.

Marinate: to let food stand in a marinade to season and tenderise.

Mask: to cover cooked food with sauce.

Melt: to heat until liquified.

Mince: to grind into very small pieces.

Mix: to combine ingredients by stirring.

Monounsaturated fats: one of three types of fats found in foods. It is believed these fats do not raise the level of cholesterol in the blood.

Naan: a slightly leavened bread used in Indian cooking.

Niçoise: a garnish of tomatoes, garlic and black olives; a salad with anchovy, tuna and French beans is typical.

Noisette: small 'nut' of lamb cut from boned loin or rack that is rolled, tied and cut in neat slices. Noisette also means flavoured with hazelnuts, or butter cooked to a nut brown colour.

Nonreactive pan: a cooking pan whose surface does not chemically react with food. Materials used include stainless steel, enamel, glass and some alloys.

Normande: a cooking style for fish, with a garnish of prawn, mussels and mushrooms in a white-wine cream sauce; for poultry and meat, a sauce with cream, calvados and apple.

Olive oil: various grades of oil extracted from olives. Extra virgin olive oil has a full, fruity flavour and the lowest acidity. Virgin olive oil is slightly higher in acidity and lighter in flavour. Pure olive oil is a processed blend of olive oils and has the highest acidity and lightest taste.

Panade: a mixture for binding stuffings and dumplings, notably quenelles (fish rissoles), often of choux pastry or simply breadcrumbs. A panade may also be made of frangipane, puréed potatoes or rice.

Papillote: to cook food in oiled or buttered greaseproof paper or aluminum foil. Also a decorative frill to cover bone ends of chops and poultry drumsticks.

Parboil: to boil or simmer until part cooked (i.e. cooked further than when blanching).

Pare: to cut away outside covering.

Pâté: a paste of meat or seafood used as a spread for toast or crackers.

Paupiette: a thin slice of meat, poultry or fish spread with a savoury stuffing and rolled. In the United States this is also called 'bird' and in Britain an 'olive'.

Peel: to strip away outside covering.

Plump: to soak in liquid or moisten thoroughly until full and round.

Poach: to simmer gently in enough hot liquid to cover, using care to retain shape of food.

Polyunsaturated fat: one of the three types of fats found in food. These exist in large quantities in such vegetable oils as safflower, sunflower, corn and soya bean. These fats lower the level of cholesterol in the blood.

Purée: a smooth paste, usually of vegetables or fruits, made by putting foods through a sieve, food mill or liquefying in a blender or food processor.

Ragout: traditionally a well-seasoned, rich stew containing meat, vegetables and wine. Nowadays, a term applied to any stewed mixture.

Ramekins: small oval or round individual baking dishes.

Reconstitute: to put moisture back into dehydrated foods by soaking in liquid.

Reduce: to cook over a very high heat, uncovered, until the liquid is reduced by evaporation.

Refresh: to cool hot food quickly, either under running water or by plunging it into iced water, to stop it cooking. Particularly for vegetables and occasionally for shellfish.

Rice vinegar: mild, fragrant vinegar that is less sweet than cider vinegar and not as harsh as distilled malt vinegar. Japanese rice vinegar is milder than the Chinese variety.

Roulade: a piece of meat, usually pork or veal, that is spread with stuffing, rolled and often braised or poached. A roulade may also be a sweet or savoury mixture that is baked in a Swiss-roll tin or paper case, filled with a contrasting filling, and rolled.

Roux: A binding for sauces, made with flour and butter or another fatty substance, to which a hot liquid is added. A roux-based sauce may be white, blond or brown, depending on how the butter has been cooked.

Rubbing-in: a method of incorporating fat into flour, by use of fingertips only. Also incorporates air into mixture.

Safflower oil: the vegetable oil that contains the highest proportion of polyunsaturated fats.

Salsa: a juice derived from the main ingredient being cooked, or a sauce added to a dish to enhance its flavour. In Italy the term is often used for pasta sauces; in Mexico the name usually applies to uncooked sauces served as an accompaniment, especially to corn chips.

Saturated fats: one of the three types of fats found in foods. These exist in large quantities in animal products, coconut and palm oils; they raise the level of cholesterol in the blood. As high cholesterol levels may cause heart disease, saturated-fat consumption is recommended to be less than 15 percent of calories provided by the daily diet.

Sauté: to cook or brown in small amount of hot fat.

Scald: to bring just to boiling point, usually for milk. Also to rinse with boiling water.

School prawns: delicious eaten just on their own. Smaller prawn than bay, tiger or king. They have a mild flavour, low oiliness and high moisture content, they make excellent cocktails.

Score: to mark food with cuts, notches or lines to prevent curling or to make food more attractive.

Sear: to brown surface quickly over high heat in hot dish.

Seasoned flour: flour with salt and pepper added.

Sift: to shake a dry, powdered substance through a sieve or sifter to remove any lumps and give lightness.

Simmer: to cook food gently in liquid that bubbles steadily just below boiling point so that the food cooks in even heat without breaking up.

Singe: to quickly flame poultry to remove all traces of feathers after plucking.

Skim: to remove a surface layer (often of impurities and scum) from a liquid with a metal spoon or small ladle.

Slivered: sliced in long, thin pieces, usually refers to nuts, especially almonds.

Souse: to cover food, particularly fish, in wine vinegar and spices and cook slowly; the food is cooled in the same liquid. Sousing gives food a pickled flavour.

Steep: to soak in warm or cold liquid in order to soften food and draw out strong flavours or impurities.

Stir-fry: to cook thin slices of meat and vegetable over a high heat in a small amount of oil, stirring constantly to even cooking in a short time. Traditionally cooked in a wok; however, a heavy-based frying pan may be used.

Stock: the liquid that results from cooking meat, bones and/or vegetables in water to make a base for soups and other recipes. You can substitute stock cubes for fresh bouillon, but those on a reduced sodium diet will need to take note of the salt content on the packet.

Stud: to adorn with; for example, baked ham studded with whole cloves.

Sugo: an Italian sauce made from the liquid or juice extracted from fruit or meat during cooking.

Sweat: to cook sliced or chopped food, usually vegetables, in a little fat and no liquid over very low heat. Foil is pressed on top so that the food steams in its own juices, usually before being added to other dishes.

Thicken: to make a liquid thicker by mixing together arrowroot, cornflour or flour with an equal amount of cold water and pouring it into hot liquid, cooking and stirring until thickened.

Timbale: a creamy mixture of vegetables or meat baked in a mould. French for 'kettledrum'; also denotes a drum-shaped baking dish.

Toss: to gently mix ingredients with two forks or fork and spoon.

Total fat: the individual daily intake of all three fats previously described in this glossary. Nutritionists recommend that fats provide no more than 35 percent of the energy in the diet.

Vine leaves: tender, lightly flavoured leaves of the grapevine, used in ethnic cuisine as wrappers for savoury mixtures. As the leaves are usually packed in brine, they should be well rinsed before use.

Whip: to beat rapidly, incorporate air and produce expansion.

Zest: thin outer layer of citrus fruits containing the aromatic citrus oil. It is usually thinly pared with a vegetable peeler, or grated with a zester or grater to separate it from the bitter white pith underneath.

Weights and Measures

Cooking is not an exact science – you do not require finely calibrated scientific equipment to cook, yet the conversion to metric measures and its interpretations in some countries must have intimidated many a good cook.

In these recipes, weights are given for ingredients such as meats, fish, poultry and some vegetables, but in normal cooking a few ounces or grams one way or another will not affect the success of your dish.

Although recipes have been tested using the Australian Standard 250mL cup, 20mL tablespoon and 5mL teaspoon, they will work just as well with the US and Canadian 8 fl oz cup, or the UK 300mL cup. We have used graduated cup measures in preference to tablespoon measures so that proportions are always the same. Where tablespoon measures have been given, they are not crucial measures, so using the smaller tablespoon of the US or UK will not affect the recipe's success. At least we all agree on the teaspoon size.

For breads, cakes and pastries, the only area which might cause concern is where eggs are used, as proportions will then vary. If working with a 250mL or 300mL cup, use large eggs (75g/2½ oz), adding a little more liquid to the recipe for 300mL cup measures if it seems necessary. Use medium eggs (60g/2 oz) with 8 fl oz cup measure. A graduated set of measuring cups and spoons is recommended, the cups in particular for measuring dry ingredients. Remember to level ingredients to ensure an accurate quantity.

English measures

All measurements are similar to Australian with two exceptions: the English cup measures 300mL/10½ fl oz, whereas the American and Australian cup measures 250mL/8¾ fl oz. The English tablespoon (the Australian dessertspoon) measures 14.8mL /½ fl oz against Australian tablespoon of 20mL/ ¾ fl oz. The imperial measurement is 20 fl oz to a pint, 40 fl oz to a quart and 160 fl oz to a gallon.

American measures

The American reputed pint is 16 fl oz, a quart is equal to 32 fl oz and the American gallon, 128 fl oz. The American tablespoon is equal to 14.8mL/½ fl oz, the teaspoon is 5mL/⅙ fl oz. The cup measure is 250 mL/8¾ fl oz.

Dry measures

All the measures are level, so when you have filled a cup or spoon, level it off with the edge of a knife. The scale below is the 'cook's equivalent' – it is not an exact conversion of metric to imperial measurement. To calculate the exact metric equivalent yourself, multiply ounces by 28.3 to obtain grams, or divide grams by 28.5 to obtain ounces.

Metric grams (g), kilograms (kg)	Imperial ounces (oz), pounds (lb)
15g	½ oz
20g	⅓ oz
30g	1 oz
55g	2 oz
85g	3 oz
115g	4 oz/¼ lb
125g	4½ oz
140/145g	5 oz
170g	6 oz
200g	7 oz
225g	8 oz/½ lb
315g	11 oz
340g	12 oz/¾ lb
370g	13 oz
400g	14 oz
425g	15 oz
455g	16 oz/1 lb
1,000g/1kg	35⅓ oz/2¼ lb
1½ kg	3⅓ lb

Oven temperatures

The centigrade temperatures given here are not exact – they have been rounded off and are given as a guide only. Follow the manufacturer's temperature guide, relating it to the oven description given in the recipe. Remember, gas ovens are hottest at the top, electric ovens at the bottom and convection ovens are usually even throughout. To convert centigrade to Fahrenheit, multiply by 9 and divide by 5 then add 32.

	C°	F°	Gas regulo
Very slow	120	250	1
Slow	150	300	2
Moderately slow	160	325	3
Moderate	180	350	4
Moderately hot	190–200	370–400	5–6
Hot	210–220	410–440	6–7
Very hot	230	450	8
Super hot	250–290	475–500	9–10

Cup measurements

One cup is equal to the following weights.

	Metric	Imperial
Almonds, flaked	85g	3oz
Almonds, slivered, ground	125g	4½ oz
Almonds, kernel	155g	5½ oz
Apples, dried, chopped	125g	4½ oz
Apricots, dried, chopped	190g	6¾ oz
Butter (shortening, margarine)	225g	8oz
Breadcrumbs, dried	125g	4½ oz
Breadcrumbs, soft	55g	2oz
Cheese, grated	115g	4oz
Choc bits	155g	5oz
Coconut, desiccated	90g	3oz
Cornflakes	30g	1oz
Currants	155g	5oz
Flour	115g	4oz
Fruit, dried (mixed, sultanas etc)	170g	6 oz
Ginger, crystallised, glacé	250g	8oz
Honey, treacle, golden syrup	315g	11oz
Mixed peel	225g	8oz
Nuts, chopped	115g	4oz
Prunes, chopped	225g	8oz
Rice, cooked	155g	5½ oz
Rice, uncooked	225g	8oz
Rolled oats	90g	3oz
Sesame seeds	115g	4oz
Sugar, brown	155g	5½ oz
Sugar, granulated or caster	225g	8oz
Sugar, sifted icing	155g	5½ oz
Wheatgerm	60g	2oz

Cake dish sizes

Metric	15cm	18cm	20cm	23cm
Imperial	6in	7in	8in	9in

Loaf dish sizes

Metric	23 x 12cm	25 x 8cm	28 x 18cm
Imperial	9 x 5 in	10 x 3 in	11 x 7 in

Length

In this scale, measures have been rounded off. To obtain the exact metric equivalent multiply inches by 2.54 to get centimetres, or divide by 2.54 to get inches.

Liquid measures

Metric millilitres (mL)	Imperial fluid ounce (fl oz)	Cup and spoon
5mL	⅙ fl oz	1 teaspoon
20mL	⅔ fl oz	1 tablespoon
30mL	1 fl oz	1 tbsp + 2 tsp
55mL	2 fl oz	
60mL	2¼ fl oz	¼ cup
85mL	3 fl oz	
115mL	4 fl oz	
125mL	4½ fl oz	½ cup
150mL	5¼ fl oz	
190mL	6⅔ fl oz	¾ cup
225mL	8 fl oz	
250mL	8¾ fl oz	1 cup
300mL	10½ fl oz	
370mL	13 fl oz	
400mL	14 fl oz	
440mL	15½ fl oz	1¾ cups
455mL	16 fl oz	
500mL	17½ fl oz	2 cups
570mL	20 fl oz	
1 litre	35⅓ fl oz	4 cups

Length measures

Metric millimetres (mm), centimetres (cm)	Imperial inches (in), feet (ft)
5mm, ½ cm	¼ in
10mm, 1.0cm	½ in
20mm, 2cm	¾ in
2½ cm	1 in
5cm	2 in
7½ cm	3 in
10cm	4 in
12½ cm	5 in
15cm	6 in
18cm	7 in
20cm	8 in
23cm	9 in
25cm	10 in
28cm	11 in
30cm	12 in, 1 ft

Index